# White Feather
# on a Bed of Nails

To Alma
Love 'n Light
Diane Trevena
X.

# White Feathers
# on a Bed of Nails

Diane Trevena

© Diane Trevena, 2015

Published by Diane Trevena

A CIP catalogue record for this book is available from the British Library.

ISBN 978-0-9933683-0-1

Cover design by Ben Hines

Prepared and printed by:

York Publishing Services Ltd
64 Hallfield Road
Layerthorpe
York YO31 7ZQ

Tel: 01904 431213

Website: www.yps-publishing.co.uk

# Contents

*Gratitude beyond measure to my Spirit Guide and Teacher, White Feather, whom patiently guided me through the many years when I was learning how to meditate and receive his transcriptions and to those Inspirers in spirit who worked with me and still help me walk a spiritual path.*

# Acknowledgements

To my Mother, Mary McMullen Trevena, thank you mam for always being there, strong, reliable and courageous. I love you infinitely.

To my father, Thomas Platt Trevena, head strong and obstinate. I wonder where I got that from.

To each of my Brothers and Sisters, for enduring the difficult times and sharing in the joyous!

To my wonderful children, Annelleise Kathryn, Ben Craig and Joshua Lee. I am proud of you all beyond words. I thank the Great Spirit that you were each born to me.

To Byron Adam, my wonderful Grandson, joie de vivre! Loved immensely.

To my dearest friend, Bob Hogg, thank you for your endless love and support.

Love in abundance to my wonderful husband, Kev, who had the tenacity to hold on when the sea got very rough.

A special thank you to the surgeons and medical professionals of the Royal Victoria Hospital in Newcastle-Upon-Tyne, who saved my father's life and whom worked relentlessly to reconstruct his face after his surgery.

Love and gratitude in abundance to my Grandparents in Spirit, Leah and Isiah Trevena and Letitia and Valentine McMullen, whose presence and love I still feel.

# Introduction

In childhood, I felt that I was imprisoned, not only because of the isolation of feeling different from my siblings, who appeared not to experience as I did, the often frightening episodes of seeing ghosts as we called them. Somewhat more debilitating, was the isolation and overwhelming sense of sadness that came from being locked in the restraints and conditioning of my mother and father's warring marriage, which at times, felt like being trapped inside a cave without an entrance. My father's penchant for alcohol made it ever less likely that I would ever be able to escape, and at times, surviving the hurt of seeing the unthinkable, was the greatest challenge of all.

After a major head injury at seventeen, when he fell down five flights of stairs on to a concrete floor in a College establishment, my father suffered a fracture to his skull and jaw and sustained frontal lobe brain damage, which was irreversible. The area damaged in his brain created violent psychopathic tendencies and his personality changed so greatly, it was unrecognizable. He began carrying a sawn off shot gun and committed armed robbery and was sentenced to imprisonment in a Borstal in London and then to Durham Prison for hardened criminals.

By his own admission he hated people, yet his fight was always one with his own self. Married to a devout catholic and raising six children in the faith, his atheism, blaspheming and cursing of Christ made it very difficult to endure.

My story is truly one about compassion, the inherent desire to love when love felt wrong and cruel. It draws upon personal experiences of growing up in the late sixties in North East England, when times were indubitably hard for many, especially for large families such as mine was, where money was hard to come by and happiness depended upon it.

Desperate attempts to understand my father's violent outbursts, and his lack of empathy or remorse led me to seek knowledge of my spiritual nature, as a way of drawing from inner strength and resources, in order to learn how to cope and survive emotionally. I am certain what aided me, was my ability to write and journey within, for throughout those tumultuous years, my journals were not only a source of contentment, but also an opening up of portals and doorways that lead me to discover the realms of spirit.

I embarked upon a quest of self- discovery, which involved me spending time with Psychologists and in counselling and hundreds of hours spent reading religious literature. I wanted to know the truth about life and about the inner core of man's heart and soul and what happened to him after he died.

'White Feather' showed up one evening some years after my daughter was born. The evening began like any other, as I sat with my note pad and pen and began jotting down my thoughts, much the same as I always had done. After a short time, I felt compelled to close my eyes and let thoughts spring to mind, unhindered by conscious censoring. It felt different from other times that I wrote. This time, my mind went blank, as if I had pulled down a shutter on all other thoughts.

At once, I became aware of a man in my mind's eye. At first the image was blurred and mutable, appearing to change slowly in to form from a plume of chalky substance, I felt uneasy, as my mind attempted to figure out what was happening. The time it took was probably no longer than thirty seconds in total, then emerging from out of the plume of cloud appeared a North American Indian, looking solid and real, with a single feather visible from out of his thick black hair. With a rugged complexion and an off-set nose, he attempted to smile at me through the plume of chalky vapor which seemed to wrap itself around us both. Though I was taken aback, I immediately felt deep emotion and tears flowed as instantly I recognized him. It was his eyes, deep set and alive with compassion and understanding as he looked steadily at me, I knew him, but I didn't know where from.

All at once, I felt my body become weighty from my feet upwards, my limbs felt like they didn't belong to me and a strange tingle of electricity coursed through my veins and my heart began to beat quickly. My hand gripped the pen and it took on a life of its own, I wrote speedily for a long time. It was as though I was aware of what I was writing and yet my mind was blank, I couldn't think of what I was trying to say and yet my hand continued to write words. This was the beginning of my channeling whilst in deep trance state, the automatic writings which have evolved over a period of ten years. These transcribed teachings form the basis of my second book, 'White Feathers on a Path of Love – Gleanings from the writings of Spirit'.

This book is a recorded account of my life, from the many journals and diaries I kept from childhood. It's a dialogue between me and my spiritual self, the way in which it was perceived and experienced and actual events that took place. The names of individuals referred to within the book have been changed to protect their identities.

The relationship between me and my father dominate the pages, and it would seem that much of my anguish was bound up within that relationship. It is true. Yet the love and pride I felt for him, which is evident upon reading, is immeasurable. When he had the fall as a young man, I believe my spirit was with him and again at aged thirty eight, when he fell from the roof of a four story colliery building and survived what onlookers called a miracle. Many years later when he was operated on to remove a cancerous tumor from his stomach, I was there praying in the hospital chapel. Then several years later, I was working in the hospital ward when they brought him from the Intensive Care Unit. His entire face had been removed because of malignant growths and a gaping hole was all that remained, where his face had once been. Many operations followed to create a jaw, pallet, mouth and nose from tissue, muscle and bone. It was a period in time of catastrophic sadness.

This exploration has taken me to the deep recesses of mind and spirit, the journeying of one's inner- self to places far beyond the reaches of the mortal world. Some may say to delve in to such hidden identities is mad enough, but to believe in it all is insane. Then I am both. Insane to contemplate that within the structure of my physical autonomy lives a far greater expression of my being, one that encompasses every living molecular structure, which shares the diversity of this planet. Only those who've ever felt the rush of excitement tingle in their veins as they witness the earth forces through the elements, can truly participate in this journey, I expect that excludes no one. Share with me.

# Foreword from a transcript from: White Feather

## The Unbending Path

'Man may, if he has the heart to look, see the vast sea of eternity and view his transgressions which have purged the natural world. Upon the tree of life, the rolling bark shows scars of a thousand years, oozing red blood tears. He may ascend to the point where land and sky meet and rest on the icon of all his efforts, upon the great marble arch gleaming like a galaxy of stars. From there he may see the unbending path, stretching into infinity, without a single point of break. Within his heart, he may know how gallant the struggle was; where man joined forces with the natural world uncountable times on that journey and sought its wisdom, and the earth loaned itself to be used in sacrifice to knowledge. As the bark peeled back layer by layer, the tree of life healed once more.

Today, the wind brings forth new seeds, and scatters them across every land, pearls of wisdom in men's hands' (White Feather)

I awoke from a dream and my conscience urged me to go back to my past again. At that moment I wanted to run, like a prisoner avoiding death, hiding in wretched caves, scrounging food from beggars, but how does one run from them self? At every turn, he is met with his own shadow. I knew then that the only way to remain spiritually alive was to return to my past, to that place of pain and sorrow and record my memories from that journey.

# Preface

Northern England bounded east and west by the North and Irish Seas, was wild and desolate, with its rugged heights, dales and invigorating coastal margins. Steeped with folklore of mystery and intrigue, the windswept moor lands provided many a bard with inspiration of prose.

The beautiful 'Northumbria', 'Anglo-Saxon Kingdom' with its patches of heath, resplendently coloured with common gorse, ling and bell heather in late summer. Hadrian's wall, one of the most notable archaeological features of Northumberland with relics of the once Roman occupation still evident at South Shields and the last outpost on the wall at 'Segedunum' (Wallsend).

On the easterly side of the county, the River Tyne, winding like a giant snake, was northern boundary of Roman Britain and had since the middle ages been economically important for the transport of coal and supplier of water to the northern industrial towns. Generations of men worked relentlessly on the Tyne, building and repairing ships until man power was replaced by heavy electrical engineering and the work force was hit hard.

Trade declined during the years between World War I and World War II, and all were made to suffer. With the closing of the shipyards and disappearance of the Coal Mines, the industrial heartland with its poverty and urban deprivation became ever more unbearable. Families went without. In 1936, a group of workers from Jarrow marched to the Houses of Parliament to protest at the lack of jobs in the area and the poverty caused by widespread unemployment.

The historically well-endowed North was troubled from long gone days. Set in outstanding natural beauty, lost in the mist, the folds of hidden combs which change with every turn, it is hard to imagine that it was once portrayed as a place of ugliness and grime.

1966. The radio played out the tunes of Marc Bolan, The Kinks, Neil Diamond, The Beatles and Paul Simon's soothing 'Sweet Sound of Silence'. Jimi Hendrix had apparently moved to England and was touring all the clubs of the European continent. It was the year Psychedelic Rock had emerged with all its associated hallucinogenic drugs, art and light shows. The film 'Alfie' had won the Golden Globe Award for the best English language film at the Cannes Film Festival. British Film was becoming obsessed with sex and class, while critically acclaimed science-fiction films such as 'The day of the Triffids' and 'Fantastic Voyage' were being screened in Cinemas everywhere.

In America, President Johnson was resuming raids on Haiphong in Vietnam, while NASA was sending its first probe to enter lunar orbit and soft land on the Moon.

It was the year I was born, from a long line of Gypsies and Seafarers of the Mediterranean, home of Pirates of the ancient world where seaborne commerce was abundant. By about the mid nineteenth century my ancestors had settled on the south west coast of Cornwall in the area known as Tintagel (formerly known as 'Trevena') home to Arthurian Legends of the 'Knights of the Round Table'. It was once spoken within our family that somewhere it is written that one of the Knights was named 'Trevena' tis' likely only to be a fable, no doubt, handed down by our romantic forbearers.

While the beautiful and dramatic Cornish scenery attracted Artists, Painters and Sculptors, my family moved to Redruth and took to the tin and copper mines which Cornwall's wealth was based for so long, some 3,000 years it is thought. In the mid-19th century some 50,000 Cornish miners were employed and when the mining industry in Redruth began to suffer in the early part of the 20th century because of competition from abroad, the last of the 'Trevena's' moved to the North East region to work in the Coal Mines.

'What heartless places they were', George Orwell wrote in 'The road to Wigan pier'. Coal Mines were places with; 'the feeling of stagnant meaningless decay, of having got down in to some subterranean place where people go creeping round and round, just like black beetles, in an endless muddle of Slovene jobs and meaningless grievances'. George Orwell wrote emphatically, having experienced first-hand the hardships those men faced daily.

My family worked hard, there was never any question about that, it was something I heard continually as a small child. A tense look appeared in my grandfather's eyes whenever he spoke of those endlessly long days in the pit.

The family were not only miners, many were teachers and scholars with a flair for competitive sports. Not only was there a blood tie which connected them, it became apparent from stories I heard, that there was a commonality which existed between many of them, an inherent energy; an unusual quirk of character, which bound them in an inexplicable way. Some might say it was a bad temper and be done with. Perhaps. Though I believe it was more to do with the artistic temperament vying for control, a fire in the soul that drives one to be all that they can be, to achieve all that they can achieve, from where it is borne no one can be sure.

# Chapter One

## *Seeds of Spirit*

It was a cold, ugly sky that shrouded the blackened out houses, where I lived, in a pit house that huddled together with others like ships on ice waters. Misty smoke from coal fires hung in plumes over a dirty bit of wasteland which separated the houses from the slag heaps. My pushchair bumped and rattled over scattered bits of coal, my bottom hurting with each jolt, I wailed and screamed until my lungs turned purple. We turned the lane in to our street, the socks and shoes on my sister's feet became visible as the mists lifted up on to the roof tops and up in to that moon grey sky.

On the old garden gate the number 8 was just visible, remnants of its once green paint flaked off every time it was opened. A picket fence surrounded a garden, thickly strewn with daisies and dandelions, toys and bikes, tins, pots and pans and things I didn't know the names of. I was never allowed to play out that side, as it faced on to the road. Around the back there was a yard with a high wall and wooden gate that I never got to see beyond. My sisters disappeared behind it, all three of them with their long manes of hair, flaming in the bright sunshine, leaving me and my brother in the cold long shadows. I cried every time they banged the gate behind them, stopping only when Mam picked me up and took me inside the back kitchen which was as dark and uninviting as the yard was.

The linoleum felt hard with torn bits that hurt to walk on, which was why I was never allowed to, or so I thought. Little did I know the real reason was because of the dead cockroaches that kept appearing in the crockery and under the carpets and cupboards every morning we came downstairs. Delighted the boric acid had once again worked but disgusted at the sight of them, Mam scooped them up in to the dustpan and threw them in to the bin outside, praying aloud she'd seen the last of them. During the day they kept hidden, being sensitive to light, but at night they would return, their heavily armored bodies hiding three pairs of quick little legs that could be heard scurrying over the walls and floors and every surface of our kitchen.

There must have been thousands living in the cavities and under the floors and foundations of our home and the more my parents battled with them, the more they waged war on us. To avoid standing on them I was thrust in to my high chair, the second I came in to the kitchen and handed my 'chewy' in which to quiet me down. It never failed. The stale smell of my spit on my chewy which was a bitten up cardigan, all holey and lovely, it pacified me for years. On this day I spied the cardboard boxes piled up at the front doorway, my old pram full of toys and terry toweling nappies and things. My sister's clothes were bursting out of an old suitcase which I could see was grandma's old one, its lock unable to take the strain, and my sister Clare's best pink dress was trailing on to the grass. Everything from inside the house seemed to be piled up in heaps outside. Roughly I was thrust in to my sister Marie's arms, my cries drowned out by the sound of the removal van's loud engine as it came to an abrupt halt at our gate. Dad and a burly man of similar statue jumped out of the wagon, banging the doors shut; excitement ripped through us all. We were moving. Today.

As young as I was, I felt the anticipation of leaving behind that horrible house with its army of cockroaches. Mam's face was alight, backlit by the winter sun. Her hair was thick and glossy and even though I would never get to see what was beyond the gate where my sisters played out, I was happy. The move from Grange Villa to Perkinsville was a major improvement by anybody's standards. Away from the cockroaches who had triumphed over us and beaten us out, at last I was free to roam, with an enormous garden with rhubarb and blackberry bushes towering high over my head and grasses that were taller than me. For the next four years or so it would serve us all well.

The house in itself was alright, except for the old outside toilet, which didn't have a light and never any toilet paper; just bits of old newspapers which made my bottom red raw. I would rather wee the bed, which may well have attributed to my ten year habit, than venture out at night into that pitch black hole with spiders hanging from cobwebs all over the ceiling. The toilet led out on to the back lane, which had droppings of loose coal all over the street from the grubby coal bunkers, that you were always rubbing up against and getting filthy from. From some observation, it was probably a street like most others around those parts of the North East at that time, but only after living there for a while, did you realize there wasn't another like it, at least not to my knowledge.

The occupants on either side of us were lunatics. In fact, as I think about it now, it was as if a dozen of criminally insane people had taken up squatter's rights. Those next door up were gypsies, who had been forced out of their caravan and given a house on the condition that they never parked their battered old wagon on Council land again. However, the fixture of a residency never dulled their sense of adventure; for at any one time, either one or both of them were gone for long periods and when they returned they would beat the living daylights out of each other. It was a regular occurrence of which the authorities seemed incapable to do anything about. Battles between them were frequent, and even though I could barely see above the window ledge, I would watch from the landing as, nightly, Mallory ripped huge chunks out of his wife's straw like hair. She wrestled back with him, sometimes kicking him so hard in the guts that it landed him in hospital. I peered through the net curtains at Mr. and Mrs. Charlton, who lived on our left, as they were leaning over their gate watching the blue light of the ambulance disappear. I would see a smug smile on Mr. Charlton's long undernourished face which didn't hide his secret pleasure. He had hated Mallory ever since he found his wife in bed with him. The only reason I knew that was because Ken Charlton had told my father and I overheard him telling our Mam one night when I had come down stairs for a drink of milk.

Mam wasn't a gossip like the other women in our street and would never offend Mrs. Charlton by being rude to her, though I suspected she secretly disapproved. I only knew that because she never stopped to chat to Mrs. Charlton like she did to the other women. I always wondered if anybody else knew about their 'guilty secret', as apart from anything else, it was obvious by the way she pushed her chest out and swayed from side to side. It was funny to watch her hanging over the fence whenever Malloy was in his garden pulling up his turnips, her with the pounds of flesh squeezed into undersized t-shirt and skirt. It was shocking really and sometimes things popped out which shouldn't have.

When Mrs. Mallory wasn't fighting with her husband, she was threatening to kill Mrs. Anderson who lived three doors down. Ellen Anderson had the skinniest body I had ever seen on earth, and when the two of them were flying at each other like alley cats, I swear I heard bones crack. I never knew why they hated each other so much. Somebody once said it was to do with their children not getting along. Then again, I didn't know anybody who did get along with Geordie Anderson. He was a greedy bully who always threatened to punch my face in if I didn't give him my sweets. I learnt to run, fast. Survival was crucial, and by aged 8 I had been taught all the self-defence I was going to need, but only of the physical kind mind you. Emotional resilience was an entirely different matter. Becoming a bricklayer of the emotions took years of intensive training.

There was a vulgarity in the depravity that I saw, something I was acutely aware of even as a child. I watched our neighbours hurling their awful four letter words at each other until the whole lot of them were embroiled in combat which lasted until the riot vans turned up, with sirens sounding, grinding them all to a halt; until they were dispersed through their front doors, like those cockroaches disappearing into a crack in a wall. I held my breath tightly, sometimes I whispered the 'Lord's Prayer' in the hope that our house wouldn't go up like a fire work, which was the usual for nights like that. In the half light, I pulled my covers round me and slept fitfully.

How the Seeds of Spirit were sown in to the fabric of my life at that age, I will never know, but somehow they were. In the emptiness of that broken up house, 'Spirit' managed to find me. Frequently I couldn't sleep from the sounds of yelling still going on behind the walls and I pulled my little book out from under my pillow, pensively viewing the empty page of my diary, as if lingering over a wrapped parcel. My small fingers gripped the pen and I wrote 'My Diary' on to its binder and my name on the front in swirly writing.

*'Dearest Diary, my friend. Can I call you that? Today has been unbelievable! I was given a 'special badge', not just like any old one I've had before, I mean a real 'you did amazing' badge!'*

I was taken around every class in the school to show them my book which I wrote during creative writing. Mrs. Cunningham kept smiling at me as she walked me down the corridor, as if she was amazed that I could fill a whole exercise book on just one story.

"But it's the contents," she beamed at Miss Burrows, as she opened the pages and pointed at my neat handwriting. "From only a picture, she created this wonderful story."

I smile now, as I picture her with her wild auburn curls that matched her exuberance and energy. Whenever she got lost in conversation, her head would nod, which made her curls spring. She loved literature, and instilled in me the rich tapestry of the imagination and how glorious it truly was.

*'Oh Diary, I long to go to that beautiful cottage in my story and experience that lovely room with the patterned lace curtains and meet that little girl who lives there'.*

In the depth of the night I dreamt of her, the little girl, as she stood holding a rag doll, in a pink dress and matching shoes, her hair a beautiful yellow. I knew it was her, because the house behind her was all white washed with pale pink roses that climbed up and around the porch that led to the front door; it was the cottage I had wrote about in my story. In fact, it was exactly like the one I loved to admire every time I passed by, on my way to Long Forge woods. So beautiful it was, it could have belonged to 'Alice' or 'Hansel and Gretel' or anyone of those fabled characters in the books I loved to read, and secretly I hoped that one day it would be mine. There was nothing spoken from the girl with the yellow hair, she simply held out her hand and gave me her doll.

Days seemed longer then. My ever insatiable hunger to get home and be with our Mam and write in my diary caused me real distress and sometimes it gave me an ache in the belly so bad, they'd have to send me home. On one particular day which stands out in my memory, I begged Mrs. Cunningham to see me over the road.

"My Mam will be in, she never goes anywhere," I pleaded. Teacher was never one to give in, but my innocence must've won her over.

"Well if she isn't, Diane, you will have to knock on a neighbour. You mustn't attempt this road by yourself do you hear?"

She looked at me, just as she always did when she was on the verge of getting cross. I smiled as she disappeared from view.

*'Oh friend, if you could see me doing this all by myself…,'* I contemplated what I would write later. I turned the corner up the dirt path, adjacent to the farmer's field, where one day I would live, though I didn't know it then, and edged between a narrow hedge and cut through a garden quickly before the owner rattled on his window. Strange old 'Piper Jones', I remember thinking, hearing his agonizing screeching attempts at musical notes being pitifully squeezed out of his bag pipes. Poor soul, I thought, he was never quite the same after his Doris passed away.

I wound my way through the back streets until I came to my garden, with its towering grass covering the ground. It was like battling through sticks. The harsh sun had scorched it and it whipped my legs as I jumped to avoid it scratching me. I knocked excitedly on our front door, expecting Mam's surprised face to appear instantly at the window as she wondered who would be calling at that time in the afternoon. I waited with excitement. It was such a big thing I remembered thinking, and Mam was sure to be so proud. I puzzled as I knocked harder. Again I knocked but nothing; not a sound from inside the house except for Snowy, our little Budgie, twittering from his cage on the window sill. Why wasn't she answering? My mind flooded instantly with panic. She always watched television before coming for me and our Thomas at half past three. Where could she be? I was getting frantic. I knocked again and waited, knowing by now she wasn't at home, so I began to kick the door, imagining that something terrible must have happened to her.

I remembered what our Dad had said the night before, "Mind you lot, if owt' happens to your Ma, you'll all be put in a home." Thoughts of 'Heidi', the little girl raised by her Grandfather after the death of her parents, came rushing in to my mind. I had read the novel many times. What if something terrible had happened to our Mam I feared? Dad's voice thundered in my head as I kicked and screamed and banged the door until I was red in the face and my knuckles hurt, and didn't even hear Mrs. Charlton shouting over the hedge.

"Diane! Your Mam's just gone out to see Meggie. She's coming back in five minutes!"

I slumped on the door step sobbing. She was our light, our Mam was. She shone out in the pitch black, like a gleaming orb of gold, saturating that utterly dark place. I may have only been seven but I knew the strain she had on her shoulders, she didn't have the support she should have had from our Dad. I could picture in minute detail, her face and eyes smiling and I could hardly breathe for fear of her being utterly extinguished by the black dark and her light going out forever. In sheer exhaustion I flopped on to the step in a heap of sobs.

If everything had been alright at home I would've excelled at school I'm certain, as I adored literature and creative writing and had a real flare for drama. I loved the way in which myth and magic enfolded reality and for a short space of time you were suspended in make believe. When I think back I can see that I drifted accidentally into a distant reality quite early on in life, a place of solitude and abstract symbolism, where often I spent lengthy time pondering and wondering, which to me, was a far more solid and secure place than the one I woke to each morning. Mrs. Cunningham often nudged my arm as I drifted in to one of those dreamy afternoon sojourns.

Journeying through the recesses of mind, I found solace in the times I went deep within myself, where I felt the security in knowing that there was something guiding me. It was always there, especially when I wrote in my diary. It was as if a light simply switched on and it felt like something was with me, a sort of kind and benevolent feeling, which instilled me with confidence and in that blanket of warmth, everything was shut out. I felt secure in the knowledge that everything was going to be okay.

In reality, of course it was far from okay. It would appear on the surface, that one can exist in a condition that binds the emotions in such a way that it prevents the natural and spontaneous development of personality. Yet in truth, this can only exist for so long, before a debilitating dis-ease of the mind sets in; this dis-ease of course is insecurity. I battled with it constantly on a daily basis, each time I witnessed once more my Mam's pained and worried expression when she spoke about Dad and I feared for all our existences.

"Diane!" Mam's voice peeled above the distant hum of traffic and wild bird song and Mrs. Charlton's parrot-like tutting over the fence. Surely I hadn't been sitting with my back against our door for long?

"Where've you been!?" I asked, gasping between sobs, as I looked at our John's little face, snuggled deep in his 'horsey coat' blanket which he liked to have with him, curled up in his pushchair. Silently I was wishing it was me. My chest ached from all the crying and a good hug would've been preferred to the reprimand she gave. She unlocked the door and I had never felt happier to be in that rotten house.

My sister's presence, to me always felt like magic that broke a spell. They only had to walk through the door and the grey washed out walls of the passageway looked a shade brighter. Marie was the eldest, she was our Dad's favorite, or that's what I believed. He was very proud of her being his first born and he always commented how strong and capable she was, but I appreciated that about her. She was bold and unafraid to speak her mind and was striking with her dark brown hair, which was always straight and tidy. She was lucky because Mam never had to spend ages brushing it for tats.

Ann was second oldest and prone to being finicky and particular. She looked after us little ones well; sometimes she was given too much responsibility too soon to take care of us and I felt sorry for her because I thought she should've been born in to more that she got. She looked like she could have been a child movie star with her thick curls of chestnut brown hair and heavily lashed eyes.

Clare was third eldest, sweet natured and very pretty with a mane of fair hair and freckles. She was a nervous child I remember, and at times Dad shouted at her to stop touching things over and over again, when she couldn't really help it. She was my savior as a child, in many ways, when fearful apparitions made their presence known in the night and she would let me get into bed beside her.

My brother Thomas, with his black rimmed glasses, which he wore because of an inherited squint, was one year and two months older than me. I loved how he could invent interesting things with bits of rubbish. He tinkered with anything, and I longed to be as clever at fixing things like he was. It was probably my adoration of my brother which made me fall in love with boys quicker than average.

I had loved being the youngest of the family for the five years that I was, before my brother John was born, because I got to spend all the time on my own with Mam. She'd take me to Grandma and Granddad's house once a week, which was the highlight for me and I willed for that week day to come. On Wednesdays, we would stop off at the bakery in the precinct by the bus station to buy a cake. Mam would buy me a meringue, with fresh cream, a strawberry and syrup on top and then we'd catch the bus to South Moor and I'd skip the whole way down to Grandmas.

Patterns made by the smoke from coal fires hung above the chimney pots and the burning coal always smelt lovely, as we turned the corner on to Keswick Road. Usually you would smell the aroma of Grandma's homemade sponge cakes drifting up the path; orange peel, coconut or date and walnut, inviting you all the way to the scrubbed and whitewashed door step. The back kitchen was always a shade dark, even when the sun was shining. It was cool but the utensils always gleamed, adding a splash of light in the glinting sun, as they hung in lines on the walls above the bench top in uniform, with edible goodies beneath; scones with fat currants and other delicious morsels which I spied greedily.

Mam and I opened the door in to the living room, where a blaze of yellow sunshine lit up the space, with dancing flames from the open fire, spitting and crackling and inviting. Sometimes Granddad was sitting, hidden, in his favorite arm chair but you would know from the tobacco in his pipe as it hit your nostrils instantly. Mostly on those days, it was just Grandma who greeted us warmly. She sat on her heavily patterned sofa, her face beamed as she saw me and Mam at the doorway; her skin was translucent like a ghost's and she wore tenderness like a robe, draped around her, sincerity and patience made up the fabric of her spirit. It was hard to imagine her, being our Dad's Mother, him being so rough and at times downright vulgar, but she loved him, like no one else ever could and it was evident to see, especially when she spoke about him. She saw his goodness and never judged him and I'm sure it was her deep faith in God which helped her at the end of her life when she was dying from cancer – that resilience and faith which surely carried her to her Jesus, whom she loved.

On this particular day however, completely unexpected, it was decided that all five of us children were going to stay with relatives because Mam was going in to hospital to have a baby! There hadn't been a mention of a baby until that day when she went in to labour and I really didn't know how she had been able to hide it in her tummy but more than that, I wasn't happy in the slightest that I couldn't stay at Grandma's like Marie and Ann could. Clare, Thomas and I had to stay at our Aunt's house. Aunty was a Lecturer in English at the local Polytechnic College and I was always a little shy around her. Though extremely kind, at times she could be strict and I worried endlessly about weeing on her lovely ironed bed sheets.

In a fraught week, being separated from Mam and the occasional wet bed and minor reprimands from Aunty Liz, our new baby brother John was born. If that wasn't difficult enough to come to terms with, worse still, was that Dad had thrown away my chewy, which, though I hadn't confessed to, I'd secretly missed all week and I didn't think I was too old for it, like he said I was. I can hardly describe the sorrow I felt, to find my bed empty where my chewy had been beneath my pillow. The smell of it still lingered there – my spit, my cardigan all bitten and holey and smelling lovely with sweat. The separation from it would take a very long time to get over and as the months rolled by, the lovely times Mam and I used to spend together, just the two of us at Grandmas, diminished, replaced by the crying demands of a lump of a baby.

John was a chubby baby and he could drink more bottles of milk than I dreamt was possible but despite this, the lady from the Health Authority assured Mam that this was perfectly normal and in time told her, that his shuffling would eventually turn in to walking, even though he was two. Even if I was jealous of my little brother, with the attention he received from Mam and Dad constantly, I dearly loved all of my siblings, in ways I'm not sure other children consider much at that age.

With our garden overgrown and our house, a ram-shackle, packed to the brim, cluttered with things I thought served no purpose, I, at times still felt the overriding notion of beauty as though I was able to see beyond it, somehow. Perhaps my imagination afforded me with a protection from the dark and harsh reality. Still however, there was a great sadness that lurked beneath and when life should have been easy in childhood, sadly it was filled with depravation and sorrow. Even a beautiful piano with its lustrous rich oak, which was given to us to learn, because the Trevena's were inherently talented musically, was hideously covered in cages, housing dozens of little field mice, most of which were badly deformed from incestuous breeding with each other. I recoiled every time I saw their tiny twisted limbs and hideous growths. I felt tortured, sensing their perpetual anguish and pain and loss of freedom and begged Thomas to take them away to free them by whatever means necessary.

Despite it all, the part of me that embraced the Spirit, remained strong and daily I prayed for better things to come. Just as long as we all stayed together and weren't split up like Dad threatened, that's all I wanted. I hoped that one day we would leave the darkness of that house behind and move to a home which was bigger and brighter.

Apparently, according to Meggie Smith, the Council had finished modernizing the old houses three blocks away, she gabbled to Dad one day, passing by our gate. Meggie told everybody everything, sometimes her news reached folk in the next town quicker than Royal Mail. I couldn't wait to see these houses with their nice new windows and doors and a toilet that was inside. I was filled with anticipation as I sneaked around that same afternoon with my friend Lucy. I turned the corner and at once saw the rows of copper piping and electrical wires laid out in the streets and skip loads of debris and cement adjacent to every house, it was a building site and my heart sank, unsurprisingly. Unfortunately, despondency was something I had by now become well acquainted with. Meggie was wrong again. They weren't finished like she said they were and it would be one more year at least before we got to step over the threshold of our nice new house with its three bedrooms, two big downstairs rooms and a lovely back garden that rested on a cornfield with an expanse of land beyond it. I welcomed that move like 'The little Match Girl' being invited inside a warm kitchen on Christmas Eve.

The sound of bird song would always wake me up in the mornings. Usually I slept badly because of night-terrors which had apparently began when I was two and I was often tired and didn't always welcome the early light that morning brought.

Sundays should have been quiet with only the lull of faraway traffic, instead of the loud din from downstairs and the sound of Mam and Dad's arguments. 'Sunday', according to my teachers, was a time of God's good grace, where we were to take time to reflect on that which had gone before in the week. The shops were closed and buses ran only very occasionally, so everyone spent family time together, they said. It amused me how removed my teachers were from my life.

I turned over the page of my diary to the day before and read aloud, *'Do I hate him?'*

I paused for a second remembering why I had written it. I read it again. 'Do I hate my Dad?' I propped myself up on my pillow and drew the curtain to one side, so that I could see the field and the neat rows of golden corn waiting to be cut by the combined harvester. I began reliving the emotion that I had felt when I wrote it, how yet another row had started an avalanche of incidents, like so many times before; of him erupting in to a rage that could split a boulder in two.

Of him throwing our television set through the window and punching two great gaping holes in to the sitting room door, then rolling out in to the street so angry, inviting any man big enough to take a chance to fight him with their bare fists. I rolled up my sleeves, closed my eyes and imagined socking him right between the eye balls.

'No dear Diary' I contemplated. I didn't hate him. I closed the book tightly, placing it carefully beneath my pillow, yet I didn't know what there was to love about him either. My Father was an awesome, formidable man, who had a .hunched back from carrying sleepers from the woods near where he worked, to our house, to chop up for fire wood. He shouted when he spoke and his size 10 boots could be heard thumping down the path signaling he was home. Though he had once been handsome, his good looks had been replaced by years of hard work and hard drinking. He was a scrap man by trade and everyday he got up at the first light and walked the three miles or so to the tip site, where he worked like a Trojan until dark.

I used to hang out of my bedroom window and watch for him coming. It faced on to the cornfields where to the right of them was the park, or what was left of it. As a reminder of its existence, a distant outline of a shuggy boat swing stood, once painted pillar box red where a hive of eager youths would wait to clamber on it and force its breaks, making it swing in motion of 360 degrees, with them still hanging on for dear life.

Beyond that was a clump of hill known as 'Roly Poly Hill' which led to Long Forge woods which had trees with rope swings hanging from them, daringly jutting over a fast flowing river. It was a fabulous place to live when I think back – you could walk for miles and never encounter a soul. When the noise in my house got so bad I would go to the woods and hide amongst the fir trees vowing that I would never go back, but as darkness began to creep in, I would nervously set off in the direction of home, tentatively listening for mice squeaking in the high corn. With no other way of getting back it was useless to deliberate, so with the blades of grass whipping my knees, I leapt and jumped trying to avoid putting my feet on the ground. Sometimes just as I got near home, my Dad would emerge as a tiny speck in the distance and I could barely make him out in the pitch dark but for his distinctive side-to-side waddle, as he balanced huge sacks of scrap on his back.

"Dinky!" he would shout, his rich Geordie accent a warm comfort in the dark. "What ye doin' here?"

His face beaming as he came under the lamp light. 'Dinky' that's what he called me, probably because I was the youngest daughter and slight for my years. When he was happy his voice rang out like a bell and there was no mistaking it, but if it didn't, well you knew the night was going to be excruciatingly long.

The strain our Mam was put under was something I found increasingly hard. If only the bell would ring more often, I used to think, if only he could stay that way, like he should've been, before the accidents and those things that altered the course of his life forever. How lucky I contemplated, he was, for bumping into our Mother, all those years ago.

Mam was a wonderfully quiet and hardworking woman, her whole life revolving around her family. I thank God she was as strong as she was, because her love for us was the elemental glue that held our family together. I remember as a child looking up at her whilst sitting on the apron of my brother's pram, thinking how black her hair looked against the sky, a rich raven color of coal that shone like spun silk.

She was small and slender with eyes of deepest cornflower blue and features undeniably attractive, probably from generations of her Irish descent. She possessed a quiet Catholic faith which we respected by going to church every Sunday and saying our prayers each night; and within her was a lion-heart of spiritual strength and energy – there must have been for what she put up with.

It wasn't that my Father was all bad, in fact, sometimes his stories of his own youth were so richly embroidered with emotion and pain that his grey eyes would glass over and a tear would spill as he spoke of his Mother with such love and respect. I don't think I had ever heard anyone talk with so much love, but the anger in his heart gave vent to such hurtful accusations about God and people that my Mam used to say he was eaten up with hatred and that one day God would punish him. For years he hurled insults up at the heavens, swaying from one side of the street to the other with a belly full of beer.

"Ye bastard you're not powerful. I'm the Daddy!" he would shout. He even tattooed the words on to his knuckles. "Nobody is stronger than me!" He would look up at the sky and bellow like a bull.

I would watch him stagger up the street nearly kicking the gate off its hinges as he rolled in to the passage and into the kitchen.

"Get up stairs you lot!" Mam would shout to us, banging the dining room door shut to block out their voices, but we could still hear them – Mam's normally controlled voice beginning to crack with anger as Dad protested in defiance.

"It's only fuckin' money, man!" he would say.

I squeezed my sister's hand, watching the colour drain out of her.

"Wish they'd stop," Clare whimpered, dancing on the spot, trying to control her nervous bladder.

How I detested those times, watching my sisters and brothers clamber into ridiculous hiding holes to blot out the noise; under the bed, in the airing cupboard, squeezed in behind the toilet door. I listened intently, ready for the moment I thought Mam was ready to cry so I could race downstairs and shove myself between the two of them, prizing them apart.

"I tell ya what' a'l do right? ... A'l throw the bastard money in the fire and piss off out!" Dad's voice slurred.

"Don't be so bloody stupid!"

She'd make a thrust for the flutter of notes, unable to reach them in time, they'd fall in a heap on the roaring red coals.

I watched her from the living room door, her beautiful face crumpled in total despair. "How am I gonna buy food now?" she said, as she turned and saw me. "Diane go upstairs now!" she shouted protectively.

"I can't Mam, I'm scared," I sobbed.

She turned to face him. "See what you've done!" she lunged at him pushing him hard against the window, "you've hurt them again!"

He saw the look in her eyes, as I did, as she picked up anything to hand, an ornament, scissors, whatever it might be and stretching to her fullest over him she pushed him backwards until he backed away towards the open window.

"Chick, come on man, I didn't mean anythin' by it," he said. You could hear the apprehension in his voice as she inched the scissors closer to his chest.

"Here I've still got a roll of notes, man," he pleaded, holding out the money but she had gone beyond the point of return. I knew it, because I had seen that look many times.

"Stop it!" I screamed until I was hoarse and pushed myself so hard between them that he had no choice but to flee through the open window. I watched him from the bedroom window, stumbling and falling into the tall corn, where he would rest for a few seconds and then scramble to his feet again. I'd watch, while downstairs my brothers and sisters crowded round Mam making sure she was alright and I wouldn't take my eyes off him until he was a speck in the far distance. Poor Mam, I thought. I couldn't help the tears from falling. She asked for nothing for herself. I looked at the shabby furniture in the bedroom, boxes of clothes piled on top of each other and one single wardrobe for my eldest sister. We each had a cardboard box of our own for our clothes and mine was spilling over with dresses way too big, things I had been sent by a cousin who lived in Manchester who was three sizes bigger than me.

I took a last look out the window, the darkness had begun creeping over the prefab houses, dotting to the left of the old railway line and with all my heart I wished I could make him stop. The smell of his beer filled my nostrils. I felt nauseous wondering how much more he would drink before he came back and with those thoughts weighing down my mind, I climbed on to my top bunk to sleep. I could see my dad in my mind's eye as I lay in the darkness, the robust sheen on his weathered skin and a sprinkling of grey in the whiskers of his neat black beard. It amazed me how he managed to keep it at precisely the right length and thickness. I wanted to recall the good times and I lay prizing them out of the blanket of my mind, surely there was some.

Faintly I remembered watching him one morning, a Sunday I recall, remembered because Perry Como and Gene Pitney were playing out of our old FM radio, the old favorites always warbling their disdain on Sundays. Mam was still in bed, a treat she enjoyed once a week. I wolfed down my breakfast eyeing my Dad's serious face in the mirror. I watched him as he carefully took the corner of an old bit of towel, the colour of which was indescribable; probably it had once been a pastel shade. It was as black as the roads and as rough as bell metal, yet he twisted it with precision, meticulously making it in to a neat edge as though he had done so a thousand times.

Then with the same serious intent, he spat on it and dabbed and rubbed his eyes corner to corner, once, twice, three times. He switched to another corner and ran it under the cold water tap, wrung it out and then proceeded to wipe his brow, his face, ears, neck and then spat on it again, rubbing it vigorously in to his hair. He chopped off bits of his black hair with scissors that had long lost their sharpness, resembling objects that were tossed out in house clearances on his tip.

His clothes looked the same in the morning as they did at night and I never knew if he slept in them or not. He never seemed to take a bath. The sleeves of his padded checked shirt had been chopped off because he couldn't stand being hot. Even in the worst of winters, he braved temperatures below zero in just his shirt tucked in to old denim jeans. If he possessed a coat, I never saw him wear one.

I watched him fill a plastic bottle with coffee that he had left to cool in mugs on the bench and then he cut a huge onion in half. You could smell it was hot by the stinginess that instantly made your eyes water. He ate it raw, devouring it as though it tasted delicious.

"It's good for you Dinky," he said catching my eye in the mirror, "it'll put hairs on ya chest."

That made me laugh, every time he said it. Apparently, Granddad had told him as a youngster that an onion was a medicinal curative remedy for colds and sore throats and he regularly ate it, though I doubted this was as much as our Dad did. All Dad took for his lunch-time bait was raw onion and cold coffee, which was apparently ample to sustain him until he got home in the evening when Mam had a plate of dinner waiting for him, stacked high with meat, vegetables and bread. I had to admit our Dad was as strong as any man I had ever seen and he never ailed from anything. If it wasn't for the 'Jekyll' in his character that came out when he was angry, especially in drink, I thought I had much to thank him for.

Yet tonight fighting back tears, I was anything but proud. The image of him staggering over the field back to the pub filled me anger and hatred. It tore out my heart to feel such emotion that I would never admit to possessing. I would never allow myself to feel for long what it was like to hate, probably out of fear of a revengeful God and being struck down dead by Him.

As I lay in the dark staring up at the ceiling, splattered with wisps of light reflecting from the street lamp through the window, I wished desperately that I hadn't been drilled for all those years by religious teachers, preaching their empty and endless messages about love and self-sacrifice. Or by the Priests on Sundays, who stood in their pulpit in their fineries of robes edged in gold thread, gripping their leather bound bible, fixing us with their solemn expression whilst reminding us how lucky we were, declaring that 'poverty' was not particularly a problem in our country and how if we looked at the plight of those in the third world, we had nothing in reality to complain about. Eager attempts to fill their velvet lined collection boxes. I lay smarting from the anger burning my cheeks, otherwise cold from the worn blanket covering my thin body. Once again I would succumb to the demon threatening to take control of my emotions and once again I would give in to love. I slept fitfully.

Each night with absolute regularity, I awoke from horrendous nightmares, so lucid in content that I was unable to tell if I was awake or still sleeping. Things of unimaginable grotesqueness transformed themselves upon the walls of my bedroom, whilst huge orbs of shimmering lights transformed into sphere shapes which glided closer and closer to me, until the substance they were made of, wrapped itself around me and hugged me for a split second, as if shielding me from the looming dark forms creeping up behind them. I felt such enormous fear well up inside that I yelled out with so much force, waking the whole house up.

The landing light flicked on. Dad's appearance in the doorway instantly calmed me. So he *did* come home, I thought, relieved. Whatever time of the night I awoke, he was the one who came to rescue me from the terrors.

"Ya all right Dinky, nothin' can hurt ya."

He'd stroke the top of my head and tell me to lie back down. Sometimes he would tell me silly comical stories to ease my mind, jokey swear words for monsters and things which undermined their power over me and made me feel better; but after he closed the door behind him, and switched off the landing light, I gripped the bed clothes firmly, pulling them up to my chin watching fearfully in the darkness for the return of my night visitors. As if sensing my anguish, my sister Clare beneath me, in a gentle voice told me to get in beside her if I was afraid.

"Just don't tell me what you can see" she whispered, "I don't want to know," she urged.

I climbed down from my top bunk bed and squeezed in to the cramped space beside her, which was hotter than a water bottle, and eventually fell asleep. Behind closed eyes, I sensed a protective presence even in the depths of sleep. The 'Light Beings' as I called them, their weightless bodies aglow with colors, weaved in and out of the shadows cast by the moon light, brushing past me lightly as though not to awaken me from slumber. They had chased away the grotesque forms and soothed me as I lay. Sometimes I could feel the warmth of their touch, as if a sprinkling of magic had been placed upon my eye lids and I was immediately transported to an amazing place, a place I would visit countless times in the years to follow. I wrote about it the next day in my diary.

*Hedge-grow and bluebells grew all about and purple heather sprung out from four leafed clover, washing the grasses with splendour and life. From the peak on the hillside where I stood, the air was pungent with the ripeness of summer. A spring of water trickled softly down the hillside, glistening with unimaginable beauty. Wind song had died on the evening breeze and the sky* hung in lilac shades with clouds passing slowly overhead, no sounds to hear save the rustling branches from a lone silver birch and sweet trill. I stood, all five foot of me, feeling as though I could easily fly off the sides and swoon like an eagle out over the valley to the far distant mountains, where a myriad of flowers, every colour of the rainbow, dotted the ruddy brown earth. How I wished I could see beyond the mountains, where the sun blazed a trail of neon light upon the clouds.

I felt myself become lighter with each thought as every part of me longed to leave the heaviness behind and glide right over to see what was there. As surely as I had the desire, my feet lifted off the firm bank and I began to drift ever so gently upwards, two feet, three feet. It was incredible! The breeze I had scarcely noticed when I had been standing, began to tickle my face as I floated above the ground and out over the valley. On and on I flew with ease and comfort, seeing the contour of the land beneath me. I almost skimmed the tops off the trees as I gained in speed, exhilarated, twirling round and round in midair. I passed over a forest where every type of tree clustered in their hundreds. English Elm rested her long trunk beside Scots Pine, Norway spruce coupled with an old Oak, huddled in amongst broadleaved trees with their narrow trunks reaching up towards the light. Sparrow-sized birds nested beside Grey Heron on the water's edge. I hovered to watch a speckled Wood Butterfly teeter over a Cuckoo flower, its delicate pink petals blushing crimson next to the brown and cream speckles of the butterfly's wings. I was amazed and transfixed, I wanted to stay forever'.

'What injustice'… I wrote on in my diary.

'What wretched a thing to experience, with such joy in the heart, only to be thrust the very next second in to a world of displaced entities, disfigured and tearing at my spirit to claim it as their own.

*With lightning speed, I had been hurled through a tunnel with so much force that my body felt wrenched, skin from bone. The beautiful colours of the summer's evening had gone and were replaced by lifeless shadows of black and grey. As I hurtled along, I felt as if I was getting smaller and smaller or perhaps the things around me were getting bigger, in the moment it was happening I couldn't tell. I just succumbed to the terrible force thrusting me onwards. I was gripped by the arms of such terrible creatures, being squeezed to unnatural proportions, unable to protest, all I could do was to wait until it was all over, helpless even to move.*

*Sometimes I awoke before I reached the end of the tunnel, and I would be so relieved my life had been spared, but more often than not I wasn't, and each time it was more horrific than the time before. Each time I sped along feeling so afraid that I was going to die, I tried to cry, thinking perhaps it would make it stop, but I couldn't even do that. I reached the end with so much force, I felt my head was going to explode. In an instant it was all over. I felt as if I had shrunk, that I was no bigger than a pea, all around me was black dark, I believed I would never find my way out of there, I felt as if I really was dead.'*

When day light was just about penetrating the blanket of dawn, I awoke with thoughts and reached for my diary and pen again, scribbling quickly. My writing was barely legible to anyone else and I had no idea yet of its significance in my life or how reassuring it would become in my times of distress and how one day it would all make sense.

*'How beautiful is life in this age, heartbeats of children, little children, how special you all are! Each one of you is a polished jewel upon the Maker's lantern, glowing and beaming and lighting the whole universe! If I could catch the light inside each child, it would be a myriad of colours, creating a magnificent sight to*

*behold. Pearls shining like crystal clear waters, projecting light and love to every one in every land! 'Little Children' your grace is in our keeping, may we strive for thy sakes.'*

I could not know then that I was opening up to a world of reality that was as much a part of me as the physical world I existed in my waking hours, or that my spirit sojourned in the realms of this 'outer' world each night as I slept. It would take many years of heartache for me to come to accept and understand that this was to be a part of my earthly experience, and that the more I resisted this natural incline, the harder it was going to be.

The streets of my neighborhood continued to be a source for endless fascination for me and daily my diary was filled with accounts that, too others, might appear to be fictitious, only they weren't. I found so much joy in writing about the characters that even whilst being read at school, little did my teachers realize that my stories were filled with facts about real people and I was amused when they laughed aloud. Surely people like 'old Sid Spencer' didn't really exist, did they?

I will never forget the day I came home from school one day and Sid was resting against his gate like a man about to die, with his hair and clothes caked in white chalk giving him the appearance of a ghostly apparition. Standing beside him was his old Mother, a mere wisp of a woman with the withiest face I ever saw, even in books.

She was blubbering quietly some strange Latin and I was almost knocked over by the smell coming from them – it was rotten, foist and dank like the moss under trees. At first all I could do was grimace. Then I spotted a man covered in protective overalls which looked like a space suite, holding a long cylindrical tube attached to a machine, going in to their house, pulling a mask over his face before entering.

I knew it was rude to stare, as my Mam had told me often enough. She reminded me it was a habit I had to break, unless I wanted to get in to trouble from people and of course I wanted not to. I tried to remind myself of it that day, but I was rooted to the spot, like an oak tree engulfed in the putrid stench of dead moss.

'What is that smell?' I must have uttered the words aloud.

Poor Sid had difficulty speaking. Too much alcohol had fried his brain, my Mam used to say.

"Fumigation!"

It was powerful the way he said it aloud, as if he was calling an army to attention though it didn't surprise me; it was no secret that the Spencer's house was very dirty. Even from the outside it was obvious, as the net curtains were pit black and the smell from their downstairs toilet with the window open on a summer's day was indescribable.

I suddenly looked into old Sid's eyes. I remembered thinking that there wasn't much of him left in those eyes; they looked like frosted marbles. I was right and two weeks later he was gone. The gift of prophecy by now was a valuable tool in my life, though I didn't necessarily feel glad to have it. Sid's mother baked a cake for the Funeral Wake a week later and straight after, she was taken away to a Nursing home and their house stood boarded up for months with official Council people declaring it 'unfit for habitation'. I wondered about the bugs.

If it were not for my writing I don't think there would have been any other way of expressing my feelings. I doubted others had such strange experiences, certainly no one else in my family did. As far as I was aware, there was only me who saw the apparitions and colored lights in my room or flew over cornfield and hills each night I slept, waking up convinced that I really could fly.

I knew early on, from the look on Mam's face when I tried to describe the 'Angel- children' sitting on the grass in our garden, that it would be ludicrous of me to expect her to believe me. I didn't have the capability then of explaining that it wasn't really my physical body that flew but was something else, some other part of me that seemed to step out of my skin and knew exactly where it was going. I understood perfectly that it was to be a very secret affair between me and my diary, a dialogue that would last many tumultuous years.

In the daylight hours, with the sun high overhead, I ventured across the cornfields, clutching my notepad, past the roly poly hill along a dust covered path to a large white house set back in an acre of land, surrounded by apple trees. The cottage in my story. I viewed it, like an Estate Agent might, pondering over its dimensions and admiring its features.

What a wonderful place to live, I thought, standing five feet tall and peering over the wrought iron gates which I longed to push open and run up the garden path and pretend it was home. There was never anyone about, certainly never any children, though it didn't look very hospitable for the antics of youth, as the lawn looked far too neat. I imagined my curled up toes digging in to that soft grass and smiled.

On I ventured down the winding narrow road, past two farm houses until I came to the woods, with the beating sun blazing on the trees. I'd slip through a clearing in the glade and stand upon my favorite spot. Oh how beautiful even to me then, with birdsong like a symphonic orchestra accompanied by twinkling melodies from the flowing river. On top of the world, surely as close to heaven as one could get, I'd sit and write and dream.

*'Have you ever wondered about a life beyond this life?'*

My neat writing graced the page as I viewed it later that evening.

'Or of an existence beyond all this?' it continued. 'Because sometimes we need to think about it, sometimes the things that happen to us will stir us to remember. Just like the places of serene beauty I have visited in my dreams. Where tranquil light sheds beams of warmth, neither hot or cold, covering your whole body with feelings of joy and love. Where we feel lighthearted, carefree and supported, as though cushioned by softest feathers, with ease and contentment, we glide and sometimes we fly'.

'May 4th 1977' I wrote speedily, 'I remember it like it was only yesterday. 'I am sitting on what looks like benches placed in rows in a sort of church. There are many children like me all seated next to one another. I am wearing a sky blue dress made of satin with a ribbon tied in a bow around my middle. I feel so dressed up, I want to squeal with excitement, the sheen of the satin radiant in the translucent light. I am thinking how bright everything is, the walls, with ornate coverings upon them, shimmer with a pure radiance, yet there is no sun and there is no roof. The warmth is steady and I have never felt more wonderful. I swing my legs in anticipation of what is about to happen. A Temple, I think to myself, that's where I am, a Temple of unimaginable beauty. Love is streaming out steadily from every corner, nook and cranny and I feel connected to everyone here. There is no resistance from anybody to be their true selves. It is the first time in my entire life I feel safe and secure and from this day on I long to return. I wish I could remain in this place forever.'

I don't know why I kept having the dreadful experiences where I feared going to sleep, knowing I would fall in to that maelstrom of emotions and terrifying realities. I never felt safe or secure then. Perhaps it was an extension of the insecurity I felt during my waking hours. I was often exhausted in the day time and often at Junior School, I would nip out of class and sit on the toilet and close my eyes, worrying about Mam. What if some-thing bad really happened to her, I feared? What would happen to us then? Sitting on the cold seat, staring at the washed out cream ceramic tiles, I pictured her in the kitchen, cooking our tea and all I wanted was to run home and be with her. How long I spent in the toilet I was never sure, but judging by my teacher's reaction, it was probably a great deal longer than everybody else.

The summer holidays couldn't come quick enough. What was so good then, was the feeling of community, the way in which everybody knew each other in our street, a familiarity amongst the old folk and young, whose bairns played in the gardens, swinging on the gates. I liked that, the familiarity, but even more, I especially liked that in our street there was a kind boy called Simon, he had dark blue eyes and always told me how nice I was, even though I couldn't get a brush through my hair.

As I walked down the front path of our garden, our dog Jip barked and set the neighbours baby off crying. "Jip!" I shouted, "Come on lad!" He would run up to me; he was a big muscular Labrador-Alsatian with only half a tail, which he couldn't wag, caused by being knocked over by a car. He was a gentle giant, and though he fought with the Sutton's dog up the street and always won, he was soft and faithful. He would follow our Dad to the pub and sit on the step waiting for him for hours on end, then saunter after him home again. Sometimes he got hit when Dad was in one of his tempers and took in out on anything. A punch on Jip's nose was 'just discipline', Dad told us. But I thought it was a terrible thing to do.

One day Jip went missing. Dad looked everywhere, a hint of worry flickered over his brow as all of us followed him over the fields and woods calling his name until our throats were hoarse. We trudged the streets and looked in every field and hedge. After hours we trawled back home and sat waiting, my nails chewed down to the wick, waiting for Jip to come back. Dad was starting to lose hope.

"Jip wouldn't get lost, Chick, he knows everywhere round here," Dad said to Mam as I listened at the dining room door when I was supposed to be in bed. "He's gone." His voice was low.

I raced upstairs, plonked down on the floor and cried my eyes out. Climbing on to my bed ten minutes later, I looked over the black pit of land outside, not a light to be seen anywhere, rain lashing down heavily. I felt my heart would break. Where could he be? How could I go to school tomorrow knowing he was gone? I scrunched the blankets between my fingers.

In the morning the coldness stung my cheeks. We didn't have the luxury of radiators and frost patterns had transformed the window into a sheet of intricate etched designs. Autumn had gone, with the lovely blanket of golden leaves replaced by frost. Daringly I got up and put on my clothes with speed. With a bit of luck the fire would be lit, failing that we would have to make do with the gas ring lit on the cooker. Getting round the table for breakfast was on a first come first served basis. Being younger I was usually given a place to sit, much to my sister's disapproval. I argued that I might have a chair but I had less to eat than they had, so much so that I used to have to eat fast in order to get seconds and whichever bits were left over. I couldn't have cared less that day though, my mind and heart was someplace else, with only thoughts of Jip.

School was harder than ever that day. Nobody seemed to understand how terrible it is when an animal you love goes missing.

"Maybe he's dead," my friend Mandy said.

Huh, some friend, I thought as I kicked the stones, picturing her hard expression. Mandy was a nice enough person but her charmed life made her out of touch with mine. Her father travelled away a lot and brought home lots of money, their house was posh, so perhaps somewhere within me there was a bit of denied jealousy.

Slowly I walked down the dirt path to where Jip would normally be standing at the gate, my mind reassuring me that as it was cold and Jip loved to curl up in front of the hot coals, he wouldn't be in the garden today. Pushing open the front door I strained to see in to the living room and the blazing fire with logs spitting on to the hearth greeted me with luxurious heat.

"Still no sign of him," my brother grunted as he nudged past me carrying a plate full of corned beef hash.

My heart sank. I couldn't control my sorrow, and frustrated, I threw my school bag on the floor and headed for the kitchen where Mam was slaving away at the cooker as usual.

"Mam," I said, plonking down on to the bench, "I can't carry on as if nothing has happened." I looked at her serving the heaped platefuls of food. "What will happen if Jip doesn't come home, Mam?"

I felt as if I was squeezing the emotion out of her, willing her to surrender to the possibility. What did she really think, I wondered? Did she really know if he was dead? After what seemed like ages, she turned to face me with that fixed gaze which told me that what she was about to say was important.

"Diane…" She paused and continued to stir the thickened stew before emptying it on to another plate for the sixth time, "What will be will be, it's no use worrying."

That was it, as if I was meant to feel a sense of reassurance, as though the very word of God had been spoken but her so few words left me frustrated. I looked at her for a moment, her slender frame and child-bearing hips, the lovely soft skin of her face and then around at our kitchen, which was so cluttered with dishes and pans stacked on the back rings of the cooker. She was so beautiful, she looked out of place, and she didn't belong there. She was always in the kitchen, smoking her cigarette or cleaning and tidying something, but it never looked any better for it. The old cupboard doors were desperately in need of replacing and bits of Dad's spat-out chewing gum were glued all over the tops of the benches amongst half eaten onions. Surveying the room blankly, I thought about Jip again. Okay, I reconciled. I would wait it out, but there was no way I was prepared to accept that he was dead. I was obstinate like many of the Trevena's gone before and as long as I held a vision of him in my mind, I knew he would come back home.

Later that evening, it was me who shouted downstairs that there was a big Policeman at our front door. I had seen him park his car and saunter up the path as I stood at the landing window, using the curtains as a stage for finger-puppets which I had made out of old bits of material. Seeing Police at ours wasn't unusual. Sometimes they had occasion to call two and three times a week. But that day, as my Dad was at home, and in a quiet mood, the presence of a Policeman was a little unlikely. I raced to the door just as Dad was opening it, my sisters and brothers squeezing in the cramped passage, desperate to hear what was going on.

"Are ya missing ya dog, Tommy?" We all held our breath, expecting the worst news. "A big, sandy-coloured, short-haired mongrel with half a tail?" he continued, as though reading from a script.

"Why aye, I told ya I was." Dad's voice was controlled.

"Ya never gonna' believe this, Tommy," I saw the glint in his eyes as he spoke, "but I think we've found him." he said.

The squeals from us all made Dad annoyed, he grunted and silenced us with his hand.

"How d'ya know its Jip, like?" Dad probed.

The policeman continued, flicking through the sheets of paper he was holding.

"Because the description of the dog you've reported lost, fits the one we've got at the station. Somebody reported they saw a dog down a well fighting to keep its head above the water, when we went to investigate, we recovered another dog but that one was dead."

He went on to explain that there had only been room for one of the dogs to survive and Jip had used the other dog to stand on and keep his head above the water. So exhausted, it was obvious that Jip had been fighting to stay alive for days. It was a miracle! My prayers had been answered and hours later Dad carried Jip in a blanket into the dining room and placed him under the table where he liked to curl up and sleep. He was barely breathing, undernourished and obviously exhausted. I stroked him and cradled his head for most of the night.

There was something inside me that knew I had a gift of healing. Not through my hands, but through my eyes. Something told me when I looked in to the eyes of the Angel-children that day in spring time, and watched the blazing trails of pearly-white light etched in pink hues, like daisy petals, stream out of their perfect hearts; and the speckles of gold dust that surrounded them, alive like fire-flies lighting the shadows where the sun couldn't reach. There was something in their eyes that spoke to me, appealed to me in a language only children can understand. The brilliance in the vision, the honesty, it made me wish to follow them when they left but just as a candle is vanquished, their light was gone.

When I ran my hands over his head, laying them gently on his brow, I could feel Jip relax under the warmth of my palms and hear his breathing become deeper. I knew that the love I felt for him was as good as any medicine. After two days of sleeping only waking for food and water, he made a complete recovery. Satisfied that I could make a difference through the power of love and prayer, I promised myself that I would always try to use the gift I had been given.

I felt sad though that I didn't have anyone to talk to about my experiences and happenings at home. Whenever I brought up the subject, Mam would tell me that Catholics didn't believe in such things. Usually I would follow her around the house as she made the beds prizing it out of her the reason why they didn't.

"You think too much Diane," she would say, piling the un-ironed clothes on top of the drawers in hers and Dad's bedroom. "You shouldn't worry about things like that, it'll make you ill."

There was hardly enough room for her to tuck the corners of the sheets under the mattress for the mountains of clothes and curtains and other things piled high on either side, I wondered how they even got in to bed at night.

"Didn't you ask questions like that when you were young?" I asked.

I knew I was pushing my luck. I felt her evasiveness was really a cover up for her apprehension as her body language had become defensive. She stood at the window with her hands on her hips, back light framing her wild gypsy hair, falling almost to her waist and she fixed me with her blue eyes in the hope of silencing me. Maybe I imagined it, but I sensed some intolerance in her as she spoke softly,

"I was brought up to believe the things I was taught in the Bible and it says that it's wrong," she said looking at me, waiting for me to answer.

At times like those, even with her rosy complexion she reminded me of stone. There was a million questions I wanted to ask her, but somehow it seemed like I was robbing her of her time, time spent away from the frenetic discord of a family who made too much noise.

"You've got a great imagination, that's what they said at your Parents' evening," her voice intervened in the quiet.

"Is that what they said?" I gripped the role of lined paper in my hands and secretly smiled.

I acted surprised, remembering how shocked Mrs. Ainsley, my teacher, had been that morning when I'd handed her my textbook at the end of creative writing, yet another exercise book filled. The next day in assembly she announced my name and asked me to come up on the stage and collect a 'Certificate of Achievement for Creative Writing'. The school applauded as I hurried on to the platform almost falling over my feet with nerves. I was eleven now, not eight, and such things made me embarrassed.

My attempt to talk to Mam about things that concerned me had failed and already she had grabbed another bundle of sheets and headed off to the boys room before I got a chance to ask if she wanted to hear my story.

"It's about an orphan boy who lives beside an old railway line!" I shouted, feeling completely misunderstood and utterly sorry for myself.

"I'll listen to it later, go on out to play," she said from the next room.

I threw the book on to the bed in defiance and wondered what to do with myself.

Even in the height of winter, Dad insisted the windows were left open in every room in our house. He was so accustomed to working outside in all weather conditions that if he was forced to breath in the air in a room, without an open window, it made him agitated. We thought it was more than that, we thought he was claustrophobic. I had seen him rip the living room door clean off its hinges just so he could feel the air streaming in from outside. Hogging the space around the roaring flames and not daring to move away from fear of the cold biting in to you, nights like that reminded me of bonfire night; but even with winds reaching gale force and icicles hanging from the plinths, the back door was wide open whenever Dad was at home.

Mam's reluctance to talk made me grouchy. A sprinkling of snow had turned to ice on the curtains, making them hard to the touch. I looked out the window to see Thomas in the garden below, tinkering with his 50cc Motorbike, his hands red raw. He stamped his feet on the ground to try and keep warm.

"Fancy havin' a look over the Forge?" I shouted to him.

He shook his head and turned the key, making the engine splutter and squeal alive, oil and smoke belching out of the exhaust. I wasn't in his best books after yesterday, when I rode it over the football field without asking him. He warned me in a way that left me in no doubt, that I would be half killed the next time I had a fancy to steal it without asking his permission first. He was a considerate person was my brother Thomas. He was placid and amicable until provoked, then his long fuse ignited without a word of warning and the anger in him was volcanic. It had me running for my life. I would keep out of his way for as long as possible, usually a day or two and he would settle down again.

I trawled through snow drifts some four feet deep, frozen to the bone, with my cheeks burning from the biting wind. I ran the last few feet to the top of roly poly hill, pulling up my hood to stop my ears aching. I stood at the top, exhilarated. There was nothing to see but a blanket of snow. In the distance a cloud of thick smoke could be seen making its way across the fields to the posh, newly-built housing estate, which nestled between the valley and an old bit of woodland. Dad would be on the tip today burning his copper wire. I let out a shriek of delight as I decided to head down to Hunter's field and root around on his tip for stuff to play with. About a hundred yards later, the smoke was as thick as black tar, hanging like a cloud above the rooftops. I coughed and spluttered pulling my coat over my mouth trying not to inhale the fumes from the rubber he was burning.

"Dinky! Get away home!" Dad's black figure appeared from out of the skip he was standing in.

I couldn't understand how he had seen me through the smoke. He looked like a black man, only the white of his eyes could be seen and his beard looked longer with ash hanging from it.

"Somebody's called the Fire Brigade. Tha think the whole estate's goin' up in flames. They're talkin' aboot evacuatin' the Ville," he laughed, throwing the scrap in to a heaped sack. "Ya'll have to go home, Dinky. Ya cannot breathe in this, man."

Sirens from fire engines sounded through the plume of smoke, you couldn't see a hand in front of you. Suddenly a figure appeared from out of the black smoke.

"You've got to be frigging joking, Tommy," a burly six-footer attempted to speak but couldn't for coughing. Dad's takings from his days work were quickly extinguished, the partly burned off copper wire glimmered in amongst the ashes as the Fireman sprayed them again.

"Come on Tommy" the same Fireman spoke. I could see that he knew my Dad by the way he joked and shook his head in disbelief. I knew that my Dad had been warned several times in the past for burning the rubber off his scrap and causing complaints from the locals.

"I know," Dad protested. Just then, he reminded me of the Yeti from my Mystery's Unsolved book, his hair caked in dust and ash, his checked shirt unrecognizable.

"It's the same old story Tommy, but I've got to say it, ya know ya gonna lose ya license if this keeps happening. The Police have blocked off the road down to Birtley because the drivers can't see to drive their cars."

"Aye I know," Dad said agitatedly and tied the end of his sack and slung it over his shoulder. It must've weighed half a ton, I thought.

"Dinky, go and get that bag over there will ya. It's got me onion in it," he pointed.

I could see by the look on his face that if the Fireman pressed him once more, he was going to lose his temper. The man clearly hadn't seen what was coming.

"Can ya not weigh it in as it is, like, Tommy? I mean with the rubber n' that still on it?"

I felt that uneasy feeling I always had when Dad was about to explode. I scrambled over the debris to retrieve his bag.

"Listen!"

Oh no too late, I thought, as I heard Dad's voice rise with anger.

"Don't stand there n' tell me how to run my fuckin' tip, alright? Now piss off!"

"Hey! Mind there's no need to be like that, Tommy," one of the other Firemen who had been listening argued back authoritatively. "We're telling you now we'll close this tip down if you don't cooperate!"

He was obviously more senior than the other man, his chiseled face bore a look that said he had seen a lot in his time but I doubted that he had ever seen anyone like my Dad before. I had that sickly feeling I always got when I knew something bad was about to happen. Dad threw his sack down and stepped forward towards the man deliberately.

"And I'm telling you that ya better fuck off my tip or I'll ram that hose-pipe right up your arse!"

I sprinted up the dirt path which was still under a cloud of smoke, ran past the fire engines with their blue lights still flashing and didn't stop running until I was as far away from my Dad as I could possibly get. That rank smell of burnt rubber clung to my clothes and made me feel nauseous. I slumped down on an old wooden bench at the side of the road, feeling as though my heart was about to jump out of my chest. An elderly couple with arms linked sauntered past, their conversation could be heard.

"It's damn right scandalous, I wouldn't care but he doesn't even live around here."

"Oh I think he does dear," the woman corrected. "According to Edith's husband, he lives up in that council estate over that way, but he's scruffy even when he's not on the tip. Larry's seen him in The High Crown. Says he drinks like a fish."

The man's voice was angry, his mild accent taking on a distinct Geordie slang like so many others when they lost sight of their airs and graces. "Lock him up that's what a' say, rid the rest o' us o scum like him…"

I watched the two of them turn the corner and go into the drive of one of the farm houses, set back and hidden by horse chestnut trees, their voices like chattering birds, fading in to the hollow. That's my Dad! I heard my voice inside my head scream and felt my face burn with embarrassment. I swore and screamed a dozen times inside my head and felt the anger tear me apart like I wanted to tear *them* apart for saying such terrible things about him. How I despised them in that moment. I felt the injustice of being wronged by the world for being his daughter and defending him, for loving him so much, yet all the while hating his guts.

I looked up the road and wondered which way to go to avoid bumping in to him. I had no intention of going back home yet, but at the same time, my fingers were numb and my shoes were letting water in. I wanted to pelt snowballs at the windows of the farm house and vent my anger at the old people for their criticism.

I had heard every kind of horrible name aimed at my Dad over the years, from the people in the posh estate next to his tip, who looked down their noses while muttering obscenities under their breaths to the kids who hung out by the fields, watching him walk past carrying ten foot railway sleepers on his shoulders. Mostly their reactions were amusing when I told them I was his daughter.

"You mean the Hulk is your Dad?" they would ask, as though the thought of him being a family man was unbelievable.

"What's he like?" they would say.

"Does he get mad at home as well?"

But the fan club comments had long lost their funny side. Most people had heard one or two stories where my Dad's feats of strength had shocked unsuspecting bystanders. Sometimes they had been embellished, to create greater effect but mostly they were recounted with amazing accuracy.

Like the time when a motorcyclist had ridden onto his tip and tried to steal his scrap while my Dad was buried waist-deep in junk. The man picked up a sack that was stacked with a pile of others, ready to be taken by Dad to the scrap yard. Dad had noticed him and jumped out of the skip and ran up the tip to stop him, by which time the man was about to ride away with my Dad's takings.

Without a seconds thought, my Dad punched him on the jaw, knocking him clean off his bike, then picked up the man's motorcycle and threw it, buckling the back wheel as it hit the ground hard.

Apparently the incident was viewed by a few people who later became witnesses at my Dad's trial, and I recall my Dad's glee as he told us what happened that afternoon at the trial, when the whole courtroom had been as quiet as if in a confessional box. He told us in great detail how he'd explained to the Jury about the conditions of the tip and how he spent most of his waking hours entrenched in dirt and other people's 'shit' as he called it. I winced at the thought of him buried under the tons of dirt, bags of sanitary waste and boxes of old newspapers and things I'd never seen the likes of.

Objects most people wouldn't touch even with protective gloves on, household goods which were piled precariously on top of each other, so high, that a gusty wind could easily topple them over. It was a scourge on the landscape which spoiled the backdrop of the lush green fields beyond, like a blot of ink on a beautiful canvas. My Dad could be seen from dawn to dusk, day after day. I'd seen him many times scrambling up the sides of the bank of dirt and grime, retrieving lengths of cable and bits of scrap. Sometimes conspicuous containers filled with liquid that smelled so strong you almost fell over from coughing, were dropped off by men in wagons who intrepidly told my Dad they preferred not to sign their name on the bottom of the 'authorization to tip' sheet.

He told us years later that a small amount of the toxic liquid had splashed on to his face and that he always believed it was that which caused his facial cancer. I knew it was dangerous for me to go there, he had told me often, but the thought of finding a little trinket to take home with me was too alluring, especially if it shone in the muck, like the tiny diamond ring I found; except it wasn't really a diamond. I didn't care, it was sentimental to me and I kept it in a little wooden box which I'd also found that day.

I watched Dad carefully peel the onion he was about to eat, then like an orator raising an important issue, addressing his audience, he leaned towards us.

"You could hear a pin drop," he said, leaning against the kitchen door, his eyes blazing with passion as he was about to tell us something in miniscule detail.

"His barrister addressed the Jury. Ya know there was about six men an' four women, lookin' at me and he told them that I was a violent man with a history of aggravated assaults and listed as long as yer arm all the things I'd been up for in the past, bloody pigs." (Police)

Dad stopped to pop a bit of the onion in to his mouth and then composing himself, he cleared his throat as he began again.

"They're all sittin' lookin' at me and I kna those bastards wanted to see me go down, but then it was my turn to speak. I said, I ask any man in this courtroom today, would you have done the same thing, after graftin' all day around in the muck to make a bit of money for your family, only to have somebody walk away with it? The Police told me I should've run to the nearest phone box, which is at least three mile away and ring them, by which time another man has stolen your days wages! I ask any man in this Court t'day if he would not have done as I did and if he's honest he will admit that he would."

Well, apparently a unanimous decision was reached by the Jury and although found guilty, my dad was spared a custodial sentence and the other man was compensated for his loss of bike and broken jaw and the reputation of Dad as Super-Hero lived on in the minds of the kids around the doors.

I was brought back from my thoughts, as the smoke stung my eyes and I rubbed them with my sleeve. Only it didn't help as my clothes were covered in ash. A tiny white feather glided in slow motion to the ground at my feet, its quill stuck in the snow making it look bright against the sludge made from car tracks. It made me think about the times I had noticed white feathers before, when I had been seething inside and unable to control the anger within me. Coincidence? I wondered as I picked it up inquisitively.

Once again, the distraction of it made the anger in me subside. I would go to the woods, I decided, shelter in the trees from the bad weather that threatened. Huge clouds weighted down with snow were emerging from the smoke plumes passing overhead. Excitement suddenly rose inside me; I could get lost in the snow drifts, they were bound to be deep and I rushed down the road, lost in a fusion of happiness and cloud.

It said quarter to ten on the clock when I got home that night. I spied through the dining room window. Mam was standing at the front door, nervously looking.

"What time do you call this?" She was startled when she saw me. A warm welcome, I thought disgruntedly. "Why? Have you been worried about me?" I asked her, knowing full well that she was really waiting for Dad.

"Nine o clock Diane, that's the time you get home, not ten!" I inched past her kicking my muddy shoes off in the passage.

"Straight upstairs." She turned me round by the shoulders. "You've got school in the morning."

"Aw please Ma, I'm starving," I pleaded, knowing she would relent. I could smell the bacon and onions she was cooking for her supper, a ritual she played out nightly for years. On my empty stomach I could've easily wolfed them down in seconds.

"Well, hurry up then," she said and eased me in the direction of the kitchen. "A bowl of cereal or something but be quick about it, and don't use all the milk."

I watched her blow cigarette smoke towards the open kitchen window, her head cocked to one side listening intently to the voices of my sister Marie and her boyfriend talking outside the back door. She had reason to worry, I thought, remembering the way they were kissing, wrapped up in the quilt on our bedroom floor the other day.

I laughed at it later when I had recovered from the embarrassment from having walked in on them. It was funny the way Marie gasped in shock when she noticed I was standing there. I didn't care, I had seen her kissing boys before and after all she was sixteen.

Mam's silent worries bothered me. The way she tried to put on a brave face when all the while she was worried to death. Sometimes I felt the strain was taking its toll on her health, not that she ailed much, but under the blemishless of her beauty I could see the strain.

"Dad nearly bust a Fireman in today Ma," I distracted her. "You should've seen all the smoke on the tip. They thought it was a fire and sent the Fire Engines."

"I know all about it," she said as she stubbed her cigarette out. "Your Dad came back n' told me." I looked at her questioningly. "Now go to bed, he'll be back any minute."

I knew what that meant. He'll be back any minute and punch a hole through the door, full of hell, hating God and the world!

My cornflakes tasted unsurprisingly unappetizing, I pushed them aside and went upstairs. Ann and Clare were in their beds talking quietly.

"He said he was going to kill them tomorrow." Ann's voice sounded afraid. "He wouldn't would he?" she carried on as I clicked the light on and searched under a pile of clothes for my nighty.

"It wouldn't surprise me, he never wanted them in the first place," Clare said sadly.

"But he's said that before hasn't he?" Ann asked her in a worried tone.

"What yer's on about?" I interrupted, pulling on my night clothes before clicking the light off and climbing in to bed.

"I'm not saying, just get in to bed, you're too young," Ann said dismissively.

I hated being youngest at times like this. I probed further, knowing my sister Ann would give in. She always did.

"Aw please tell me, I have a right to know too."

I knew that would do it, my sister's well developed sense of justice wouldn't allow her to keep information that involved me, partly because she felt responsible being second eldest but also because she liked to tell a good story. Clare moaned underneath me and shuffled deeper into her bed and by the time it took Ann to tell me, she would no doubt be asleep. Unlike Ann, Clare hated the long drawn out conversations at night. Her detached way masked a deep insecurity, I was sure, as I studied her many times when we talked about Dad. I saw the way she recoiled into herself and pretended not to be listening, but her actions gave away her fears, the repetition of her movements, honed to precision, one, two, three times she'd touch the door knob before turning it and leaving a room.

"She's got St Vitus dance. I knew a lad like that in our street," my Dad's voice boomed like a freight train, one night, above the noise of the television, distracting us all from our weekly 'Planet of the Apes'.

"Don't be so daft," Mam's disapproval was clear that day. "It's you, man! You've got them all nervous wrecks." I held my breath, waiting for my Dad's retort back, knowing a full scale argument could erupt any second. "If you didn't put them through this every day, they wouldn't have these habits."

I felt the shame from Mam having had to wash my sheets for the third time that week, a faint acrid smell of urine still lingering on them, as she carried them in off the line. Dad jumped up, tripping over Jip in the passage, causing him to yelp. He shoved open the dining room door, pounding it against the wall nearly taking it off its hinge. Cups smashed in the sink and he ranted and raved every four letter word imaginable.

The quiet of the room brought me back to the moment.

"Well, are ya gonna' tell me then?" I appealed to Ann in a raised whisper as I could hear Clare was fast asleep. "Tell me," I insisted "Before our Marie comes up."

But it was too late and a second or two later, the silence was broken by the sound of Marie's sobs and Dad's thunderous voice outside. I jumped off the top bunk and ran to the landing window where I could see Dad swaying under the lamp-light his clenched fist thrust under my Sister's boyfriend's chin. Mam shouted from the top of the step for Dad to stop, which started Jip off barking. Every light in the neighbour's kitchens flickered off, their interfering faces peering through nets to get a better view of the show.

I clambered into bed again, with my heart beating faster than a kitten's. I liked Peter. Dad had no right to try to punch him. I lay down, the sounds of shouting mixed with my sister's sobs boomed up the stairs. I wanted to punish Dad, I wished I could, just enough to make him feel what it was like to be on the receiving end. Nobody ever stood up to him. Mam tried but it resulted in such terrible arguments that I often wished she didn't. But I vowed I would one day, I would stand up to him. In that tatty little boxed room covered in T-Rex and Bay City Rollers posters, I vowed that one day I would punch him so hard he'd be sorry.

I knew how to fight. He had taught me. I pictured his face when one day, I had punched him in the stomach for the third time.

"No Dinky, yer have to punch harder that that! Go on, yer won't hurt us," he encouraged me as he sucked in his stomach, anticipating the next blow.

He taught me to curl my fist up tight so that the flat bit of the fingers made impact and to twist into his stomach so that it hurt more.

"That's it Dinky!" He laughed as I landed him a smacker. "You punch like that and yer'l knock somebody's teeth out." he said proudly.

I'll show him one day, I thought to myself as I blocked out Marie's sobs from in the bedroom as I tucked my head further in to my pillow, a deep sigh of retribution dissolving the voice of reason. I slipped off to sleep and once more in to the cocoon of the spiritual realms.

'The moonlight patrolled the glades, hawthorn, elder and willow trees held each other's fingers against the sky, wing beats of woodcocks slowly flapped as they landed in their nests, next to where I was hovering still. I could smell the woody husks from the kernels she was carrying to her young, leafy litter on the ground pattered from debris being dropped from above. With intention to *see beyond the woodlands, I am at once there, standing upon the banks overlooking the valley as it rests in complete tranquility, the wind calls for all to be quiet, to await with anticipation. At once, with almost timed assurance, like crystal threads of light, 'they' the 'Light People' appear above the surface of the earth's floor, one by one they hover momentarily, before becoming their human form. Too magical a contemplation, with faces illumined gold as if lit by the moon, dancing with aspiring grace, they become one with the elements of earth.*

*How can one imagine? Too unspeakable to contemplate, that in return, the very hands of the earth would grasp and strip and tear at this silvery light, this birth to claim as their own. Too harsh to ever witness, that every soul of mankind would manifest itself within the ether, transfiguring upon the very blueprint of life, to take at least some part of this spectacle, this thing which comes shrouded in light. With the elevated comprehension of another world, these 'Light Beings' would not deny humanity, so greatly starved, a part of themselves, for to save at least one from the poverty of ignorance will magnify the consciousness of all.*

*From the banks of the hill, I watched, as one slipped quietly in to the stirring wind, lost by the infusion of itself within the shadows and the light and was blown precariously out of the valley forever.'*

Pushing my diary beneath my pillow I could still picture the face of the 'Light Being' as it slowly faded in to the grey mist of th astral plane.

That morning, I was sent home early because of heating failure due to the bad weather. Half way up our street I heard the familiar voices of Mam and Dad, arguing. Molly Appleby lowered her head from my gaze, as I stomped past. I was quite adept at fixing people with my glare. I developed it in my ninth year. I pushed past a couple of nosey kids surrounding my gate and nervously turned the handle of the passage door in to the kitchen. Everyone was in there except Mam and Dad, who were arguing out the back. Clare's face was bright red from crying, Ann was hugging in to her, Marie was holding on to little John who had tight a hold of his Horsey Coat for comfort and Thomas was pacing up and down wringing his hands in worry.

"Aw Diane," he said when he saw me. "He's killed the rabbits, said we didn't look after them properly anymore so he's killed them."

Clare looked dreadful; they all did, in fact. I felt vomit come up from the pit of my stomach, tasting revolting. I didn't dare contemplate how he had killed them for fear of actually throwing up. Thomas volunteered the information anyway.

"He bashed their heads off the side of the shed," he said between sobs. "He did that! Can you believe it! Can you?" he repeatedly asked.

I saw the stained windows of the shed, traces of fur stuck to the globules of thick, jellied blood. Of course I could believe it. I shuddered, suddenly feeling icy cold. I could believe anything with him, remembering the time I came home to find our cat Lucky's kittens drowned, floating in a bucket by the back door and Dad shoveling muck and digging a pit by the hedge to chuck them in to. As well as a time when our neighbour brought his polecat to fight Dad's ferret. The poor creatures bit and tore in to each other's neck, until the loss of blood made one of them die or give in with sheer exhaustion. I think it might've been that day that I suspended disbelief indefinitely.

Getting out of that house was the only thing to do. Paralyzed of any emotion, I walked the four blocks in a complete numbed daze, as I took the long way round to Bernadette's house. Half way up the street I bent over, as the sick came, almost choking me on its way up. It felt like I had just climbed my way out of hell, then stepped back in to somebody else's life. I didn't know how I was supposed to feel or react. I wasn't sure if I could ever go back, knowing what was in store. Guilt drilled itself inside my thoughts. If only we'd fed them that morning. I felt warm, salt tears sting. I shoved the terrible wave of emotion away, scared that it might actually drown me, it was so huge. With each step an effort, I made my way across the prefabs, where concrete houses stood by the roadside.

My friend Bernadette lived in a council house much the same as mine. She was one of six like me. Her Mam and Dad sometimes had spats, she confided but that's where the comparisons ended. I loved to spend time at hers, it was alive with activity with her Mam busy baking in the kitchen and her Dad with his feet up nursing her baby brother on his knee, loud music descending from her elder brother's bedroom. People came and went and nobody seemed to bat an eyelid, certainly there were never any big confrontations, which made it refreshing to say the least, but it wasn't only that which I liked about her house.

It was her bedroom I liked best of all, it was lined with shelves, full of dolls, books and teddy bears just like a Victorian toy shop. She had a dressing table with pomanders hanging from the drawers, which smelled like palmer violets. Little bottles of perfume and ornaments stood on top of a book case, lined with all of my favorite fables and stories, which stood next to the window, "The Water Babies', a new one," I smiled, touching the pale blue cover. Lovely, I thought to myself.

Her wardrobe was full of fashionable clothes, many of which her mother had made. There were party dresses of lace and velvet and matching shoes and costumes for different occasions. I studied the green lining of her witch's cape, studded with sparkling stars and moons, remembering how fantastic she looked at the school Halloween disco the year before. Her costume was by far the best, everyone had agreed, deserving to win first prize – a great big soft teddy bear which sat pride of place on her pink satin duvet.

"You can borrow anything you like," she smiled at me through the dressing table mirror where she sat coating her lips with a shiny pink lip-gloss. "Some of those things are way too small for me now," she said, as if sensing my wistfulness.

"It's okay," I replied in a tone of voice I hoped didn't reveal the emptiness I felt.

I was a proud person, though I didn't know what of exactly. I didn't want to let anyone know about the squalor and reality of my life. I wistfully eyed the array of lovely things about the bedroom and secretly wished my life was like my friends. I never had the experience of inviting friends round for tea the way Bernadette did. The house was too shabby, scruffy in fact. Not that it should've been, with all the effort Mam put in to cleaning it every day, only to be spoilt by Dad's messy clothes, often thick with mud and dirt from the tip. He didn't seem to think it necessary to change his clothes when he got home from work. All sorts of nasty things dropped off him all over Mam's lovely vacuumed floor. I trained my mind away from 'that house' as sick still threatened to come up from my stomach, which ached badly as if I'd been kicked.

Bernadette handed me a pink lipstick. "You can have this one if you like, it doesn't really suit me," she said. I half managed a fake smile, taking the shiny pink lipstick from her.

I liked Bernadette. She was so thoughtful, ever since she made that first tentative remark at infant's school when she reached and took my hand.

"Will you be my friend"? She had asked, noticing that I was standing all by myself in the playground.

I knew from that moment we would be firm friends and we were, joined by the hip through infants and juniors, arms linked as we skipped down the dirt path to the neat, newly-built St. Anthony's Catholic school which nestled behind a column of elm trees and flower beds; which always got trampled underfoot whenever the bell rang at quarter past three.

There was very little I didn't know about Bernadette Doyle. With her warm-hearted nature, she was like an open book. I told her as much as I dared about things I feared she wouldn't understand and she listened attentively, sometimes prizing the hidden out of me; those dark worrisome things lurking at the back of my mind. We were like sisters in looks, people had often commented, though my hair was mousey brown, hers was strawberry-blonde with a matching pale complexion.

"It's because of asthma," she used to tell people, when they queried why she looked so white.

The poor thing, I used to think, as she always needed to stop during cross-country running and use her inhaler. I felt sorry for her because she wasn't allowed to take part in Sport's day even though she was faster than me at the relay race.

"Do you want to talk?" She interrupted my day dreaming, as I sat mindlessly stirring the red hair dye she was about to put on to her hair. I glanced up quickly, catching sight of my reflection in her dressing table mirror, it momentarily surprised me. Was that really me, I wondered?

I looked like a boy with my school blazer hiding my long pony-tail-tied hair. Bernadette had caught me by surprise and I didn't know what to tell her. My skin looked translucent with pink thread veins visible on my cheeks. I looked skinny and tired.

I could almost feel the tears stinging the corner of my eyes, my mind whirled, desperately thinking of something to say to her. How on earth could I tell her this? I scrambled a few thoughts together.

"Bernadette," I began tentatively, peering at her through the mirror. "I don't really want to talk…. I think I would prefer for you just to make me up nice with make-up and everything... if that's okay." I spoke quietly.

Bernadette smiled lively and nodded. Her eyes lit up just like sparklers on bonfire night.

## Chapter Two

# Roots of Spirit

The lead up to Christmas was the best that year. I was thirteen and blooming with youth's adornment. I was graced with good skin and looks, as some would say and though I didn't have the latest fashions, still having to make do with my cousin's hand-me-downs, I still managed to gain the attention of the local heart throb. Youth club was a nightmare. I don't know how I lived through it, soon realizing that my fashion attempts were the laughing stock of our town, amongst the teenage population that is.

The Eighties was a magical time for fashion statements and I loved it all, the lace and frills of the 'New Romantics' I tried so hard to copy and the new wave of 'Punks and Mods' screaming out their individualism. I raked through my cardboard box in frustration, desperate to find something with a modicum of taste but it was hopeless. I slumped down on the floor in frustration as the radio played out the top twenty. I pictured my friend in her streamlined pencil skirt and fashionable shoes, leading the rest of us in some weird and wonderful dance to synthesizers pounding out of speakers, ready to explode and all the girls in my year with their out-of-this world haircuts, sipping coke laced with whatever spirit they had pinched from their parents cupboards, eyeing the DJ.

I regretted telling my friend I would meet her inside now, as I nervously pushed open the door leading into the disco. It felt like I had been trapped in a beam of headlights like a frightened animal, standing there with glitzy head-band and matching belt I had created out of a curtain tie back, hair back-combed and thick black liner penciled under my startled eyes. I searched through the strobe lights for a familiar face and could've cried when I realized I was early, suddenly feeling ridiculously overdressed.

Perhaps it was jealousy that made the local girls bully me, the way the DJ showed me interest and asked to walk me home. It clearly wasn't because of my array of fashionable clothes. Sometimes their merciless name calling reduced me to tears, but always out of sight behind closed doors, when I would throw my box of clothes all over the room and rip up my oversized dresses. It was useless having pride, whatever shred of dignity I had was robbed by the reality of the situation. It was pointless complaining because I knew my parents had no money and it was futile to ask for something they couldn't give. I consoled myself by admitting that whatever it was I had, which had attracted the best looking boy in town, it was something other than physical appearance. So, eyeing the lime-green trousers on the floor I resolved to wear them to the next school disco, teamed with funky sequenced belt, and my sister's granny's shoes, I felt much better. I settled on my bed to write in my diary.

'Man shares a fundamental Truth and however the bridges form, that separate him from his true identity, one thing remains; it is his need to Express and to 'Be' and find 'Meaning to his Life'. It is the quest of the soul, the driving power that possesses him, an overriding and compelling feeling. Aliveness is the basis for all his life experiences. It is the spiritual bricks and mortar of his being. Yet why, when life holds much excitement, does man feel so unfulfilled? Is it because his sense of being alive is diluted by the events of the journey? The pushing and pulling of physicality *is to the soul, bombardment from his true goal. But what is it? What is it that man seeks to uncover within life, that it seems no amount of drawing from life's adventures distils this greatest wish? He does not feel alive to express and to feel. It is as though his body were being operated by a series of buttons being pressed. He feels out of control by the great tidal wave of living within a materially motivated world. Inertia has struck at the very core of his being. Bridges separate Mankind, they represent the ever growing Ego, they continue to build and give man a false sense of security within the world. When he might try gazing in, he is forever looking out and what he sees is a place where he knows he can never truly be free. Within every situation somewhere, there is the opportunity of unlimited potential for expression of being, the situation representing the needs within, to offer itself to that moment of life.*

*Unrest remains as the seat of unfulfilled dreams'*

I looked over the page of writing, barely legible and not nearly as neat and tidy for my usual style. I examined its content and it surprised me. I took great pride in keeping my diaries beautifully presented, therefore I couldn't work out why I felt this overwhelming urgency to write with such speed and create a mess in my book. The philosophy I was writing seemed beyond my years and yet, it was only at certain times, that I wrote this way. Each day when I got home from school, before doing anything else, I made sure I wrote an entry for that day and again in the evening before sleeping. Much of it was childish fantasy and hopes and dreams for the future. My curiosity of boys often dominated the pages, daringly fantasizing about what my first lingering kiss would be like.

Yet what I first noticed when I began writing this philosophy was the change in the atmosphere of my bedroom. I had long got used to switching off from the violent arguments going on down stairs. It wasn't difficult for me to 'slip off' to a place within my imagination where there was complete quietude and there I would absorb the peace. More frequently however, I felt a certain change in my surroundings as I drifted off to that tranquil place. I suppose I would describe it as a 'letting go' feeling. I could sense, rather than see, the green of the meadow and the softness in the pale blue of the sky. One part of me knew I was sitting on my bed, yet the other was completely immersed in this 'outer' or 'other reality'. If I allowed myself, I could actually travel in this other place, yet always I was more strongly linked to my room. I could tune in and out at will, one moment sensing the warm sunlight and the next my Mother and Father shouting at each other downstairs.

As my writing became more comprehensive and discussed areas of life I had no real understanding of, I noticed that each time I put pen to paper, a presence entered the space where I sat. It was a strange feeling at first, I remember. I couldn't make out if it was above or to the left or right of me. It seemed to occupy the whole space from the top of my head to the tips of my toes. On an instinctive level I knew this was something outside myself, it wasn't emanating from within me. It felt peculiar at first, because my whole body seemed to resonate with a high pitch sound, which buzzed in my ears, a feeling that didn't last long, perhaps only momentary and then I would feel wonderfully peaceful, nothing seemed to matter in my life at that moment.

The fearful anxiety of worrying about Mam and Dad dissipated in the cloud of contentment. Whatever it was that gave me that feeling of great peace also instilled within me a greater love for life and a commitment to honor the spiritual self. In the years to follow I would come to know it as a friend in periods of intense loneliness and a teacher to my stubborn egotistical self.

Christmas tree lights twinkled in every window, a splattering of snow fell upon pavements, making sheets of ice even more slippery as I slid the two blocks from my friend's house to mine, stopping to crack some ice which had formed on a pool of slushy water. I was feeling elated, a wonderful sense of satisfaction that I was going out with the most sought after boy in town.

It was Christmas Eve. Things could not have been better. I skidded to a halt at our gate to see Mam sprinkling salt on the path.

"Pointless doing that, Mam," I said, sliding down, grabbing on to her to steady myself.

"Get in its cold," she said as she lifted the door mat and shook it, chucking bits of muck on to the soft snow.

Inside the house was quiet. Mam's face bore a worried expression. I looked about for Jip, he was old nowadays, and his coat was dull and coarse. I spotted him in the passage way, his breathing was labored and shallow and though I didn't know it then, it was going to be his last Christmas.

I pushed open the door to the living room, everyone was there. Carol singers implored from out of the television set, the fire was crackling with splinters from the damp wood that spat on to the hearth and Mam put up the fire-guard and sat down cradling her hands round a hot mug of tea.

"What's wrong, Mam?" I placed my arms round her shoulders, nuzzling in to her neck.

"Sh!" my brother said, looking at me crossly.

Tut! "Well that's nice I must say, I've been out all day," I argued back.

"Shut up, man!" Thomas glared at me. "Can ya not see Mam's sad!" he said.

I could now he had pointed it out but I knew it was no use asking why. Clare followed me upstairs to our bedroom.

"Great isn't it," I said pulling the curtains apart to look at the frost patterns on the window. "It's Christmas eve, Clare." I turned to look at her, the soft blueness of her eyes framed by golden curls trailing on to her shoulders.

"It's not just about Dad." She spoke as if reading my mind. "Uncle Pat is in hospital again, they don't think he's gonna' live."

Her words cut me to the quick. Uncle Patrick, Mam's oldest brother who just last week sat on our settee taking small shaky sips out of his cup of tea.

"Where's Dad?" I asked, but I could see by the look on Clare's face that she didn't know.

So Mam couldn't visit her brother, because Dad wasn't there to take her? My mind reeled, I felt hopeless at the situation.

"Is he in the boozer?" I asked.

Clare shrugged. "Mam doesn't know where he is, thinks he might've gone to Carlisle," she said.

It was unlikely, I thought, as I felt the disappointment rise up in my chest. Surely he'd never visit his brother in Cumbria on the spur of the moment, unless something was wrong; but even then, the weather forecast warned of more snow to come, and just in case he'd forgotten, it was Christmas Eve! I almost spat the words out with temper at the irony of the situation. How could this sort of thing happen? Mam's brother dying of cirrhosis of the liver and his drinking partner was probably locked up in some dingy cell in Consett where two feet of snow had fallen blocking off roads, meaning he couldn't get home for Christmas even if he wanted to, which I doubted very much he did anyway!

"Come on Diane," Clare cajoled, breaking the spell as usual with her sympathetic smile which always touched my soul, "let's hang up our stockings and watch some telly."

Val Doonican was singing soulfully 'The Little Drummer Boy'

which he peeled out in a voice as rich as plum pie. I remember because it became my all-time favorite Christmas Carol and to my mind, no-one sang it more sincerely than him. I was mesmerized. Watching him sitting on his plush sofa with his hot mug of cocoa, surrounded by a hundred twinkly blue star-lights and a choral of pretty Carol singers dressed in cute Santa-Claus dresses, trimmed with white feathers, it made my heart glow with the spirit of Christmas.

Above the noise of crackling damp wood spitting on to the hearth and kind Mr. Doonican's persuasive plea to join him after the short interval, I watched surprised as the headlamps from my Dad's van shone on to the living room walls as he pulled up in the street outside. I jumped three feet in the air.

"Yes!"

Clare and I twirled around the living room in a sort of nervous frenzy. Now Mam would get to see her brother and we could celebrate Christmas as a family! Thomas joined in, wringing his hands excitedly, as he did whenever he got nervous. As soon as we heard the back door open, we fell as silent as mice waiting for the ringing out of his voice, signaling that all was fine.

"You lot!" he bounded in to the living room happily, "Here I've got some little bottles of Baby-sham for you all and Advocate for ya Ma!"

He grabbed her round her wasp waist and cuddled her, pushing his nose in to her cheek. She writhed and squirmed out of his grip defiantly falling in to the arm chair.

"Howay, Chick." He pulled at her wrists to stand up. "Let's have a little Christmas dance."

Mam's face remained expressionless through his jovial cavorting. I tried not to laugh. It was difficult though because if nothing else, the situation bordered on Pantomime.

"Dinky, here!" Dad thrust a miniature bottle of Baby-Sham into my hand, "It'll put hairs on yer chest," he said laughing.

I looked on, noticing Mam's sullen expression, searching for reassurance that it was alright to take the miniature bottle of alcohol. It was tentative moments like these that I became acutely aware of the danger from exposing too much emotion. Like intrepidly step-toeing in a field full of live mines, in a single flash it would all go up. I learned early on, it was always better to stand still and bare no hint of the maelstrom of the emotional storms going on beneath the surface. Just then Mam's face softened as if reading my mind.

"It's okay," she said smiling.

Phew. I began to breathe again as my heart restarted.

The sides of the paths were deep in powdery snow and the roads were solid sheets of black ice. Even the snow-ploughs were finding it difficult to grip them. It was a painstakingly slow journey all the way to Shotley Bridge Hospital, which I regretted the instant we had set off. All the weather warnings were being given to stay at home unless it was absolutely necessary to venture out. I couldn't feel my fingers or toes when we reached the main gates of the Hospital an hour and a half later. Worse still was the smell of Dad's half eaten onion stuck on to the back-side of my one and only pair of denim jeans and it dropped off as I staggered out of his van. John's voice chattered like a birds, down the corridors of the Victorian pre-fabricated hospital, with its cold hard floors of grey stone and lingering smell of Iodine that seemed never to leave your nostrils once inhaled.

A pretty nurse was standing by the bed of my Uncle Pat when we pulled the curtain back on his cubicle. She looked a little startled when the four of us entered, carrying a heavy cloud of freezing cold night air about us.

"It would probably be better if the children waited outside." She nodded in my Uncle's direction with an air of solemn repose on her delicate pretty face.

I felt my heart fall heavily in my chest. I knew that look, I had seen it before, on the face of the Doctor the day we went to say our last goodbyes to our Granddad McMullen. He looked exactly like my Uncle did now, lying on his back, his skin melting into the colour of the off-white bed sheet. I waited in the corridor with my younger brother who had fallen silent now, which was a reprieve. What a dark and depressing place to end your days, I imagined writing in my diary later, if I got the chance, which I hoped I would. No warm sun-colours painted upon those walls to look up at and lift your spirits, in the dim light of an endlessly long night. No soft, textured covers to squeeze in your palm, as if holding a loved one's hand. Not even avoidance from nosey visitors craning their necks to take a last look at you before you snuffed it.

My cynicism lifted off the page in petulant defiance. I vowed to change the situation for my Uncle somehow. I was so fond of him and I wanted to see him one last time. I could feel the determination in me but by the time Mam and Dad reached the end of the corridor where my brother and I stood waiting, my determination ebbed away quicker than bath water. It was too late, he had passed in to the World of Light.

Dec 24th 1980 ~ I wrote rapidly that evening in my diary.
*'Time turns gently the hands that sweep in aspiring Grace,*
*And in to the mirror appears an Angel's face.*
*Following a pattern with watery eyes,*
*Hollyhock tossed far in to the skies.*
*Forever does not mean that the seasons won't come,*
*Or that the birds won't go heavenward in distant roam,*

*For however afar you decide to go, the hands of time keep pushing you onwards.*

*Make no mistake that life kept you up,*
*Even when hardship turned a moment into a lifetime.*
*Tis' the Creator's own way of keeping you here,*
*For Golden is the Light around every Sphere'.*

*'Christmas Blessings to our Dear Uncle Patrick McMullen and a long goodbye to Jip.'*

I don't know whether we can ever really know for sure why 'it' happens or even when 'it' happens, with any certainty. All I know is that one day you walk out the front door and turn a familiar corner in your youth and suddenly all at once everything has changed. The road forks ahead in exactly the same way it always has done at the end of the street, with the same street lamps off, despite complaints from residents tripping over the unleveled paths, on their way in and out of the local Social Club. The arguments from number eleven, our house, are as heated as yesterday, last year and the year before that. But something has changed. Indifference. It just slipped in the back door and rolled you out on the pavement with a large bag of egotistical pie in one hand and a mighty great stick in the other.

## Chapter Three

# Growth of Spirit

"Diane!"

I could feel the soft dew of the sea-campion and rock samphire growing on the cliffs. It was cold to the touch and I could feel the sea fret spitting on my face from the groaning ocean waves beneath but I couldn't see anything in the lost mist, just my name I could hear being called over and over again. I felt someone standing over me, perhaps it was my imagination but it felt comfortable. I wasn't afraid. My head rested on a shelf of gala rocks, a feeding spot at low tide for thousands of sea birds. I had been here many times with the sea boiling even on the calmest of days.

It was a good day, a lucky day with a big azure sky, even with night falling on the endless wall of cliff you could still make it out. I would rest here a little while and dare to float over the edge, perhaps stopping a moment or two to look at the sea hold daffodils and bluebells that were scattered in the folds of hidden combs' and maybe stumble upon unwary Mariners there.

*"What is Death? A fathomless sea? The Great Cavern of emptiness that engulfs every single thing that enters it? Is it the purest place of sanctuary where every heart has to pass, in to the still water for purification? A pool of endless light, that rises up as you gaze into it?"*

The faceless stranger standing over me was speaking gently, his voice soft like musical notes. I didn't ever want to stop listening.

All at once, like so many times before, I felt myself being pushed hard, this time off the cliff. My heart thumped so hard I actually thought it might stop. I awoke in the half light of early morning, gripped with a foreboding sense of dread and deep sadness. I couldn't distinguish where at first I was, until I saw the pale cream of the walls in my bedroom. Glad to wake up, I surveyed the patterns made by cobwebs on the ceiling. I would think of something pleasant, anything to drive the fear of those dark shadows away. Yes that's what I would do, I would think about love.

I was sixteen and I was in love, I was sure I was. I wanted to shout it aloud! Well I was certain it was love by my diary's entries, which were full of childish hearts and kisses with cupids bow going right through both our names, joined in swirling italic writing. I viewed the last few entries, re-reading them over and over with tingling excitement. The whole thing had been like the whirlwind that took Dorothy's house in 'The Wizard of Oz' right up in to that torrid sky.

In six weeks since my Birthday I had met a boy who was three years older than me and who had all the maturity of someone who had lived an interesting life and had manners, which were missing from the boys around the doors and to tip the scales he also had a car, which meant we could go and see all the beautiful places I dreamt of. There wasn't any question we weren't going to be together forever. Romantically, I had created a picture of 'love reality' loosely based on the love affairs of the old Hollywood Movie stars that I used to watch insatiably with Mam. I had no reference of real love or anything that resembled it. Adult life for me was filled with intense drama and suffering. All I could do was re-create it, indifferent to whether it was right or not.

I tried not to think about 'Sex' even though it had happened; actually on the back seat of Robert's car, in the dense bit of woodland that I had haunted as a child. Wasn't sex what people just did? I asked myself time and again after that first furtive experience together.

I recall my first harrowing experience when I was only five years old, when the teenage boy from next door who I remembered thinking how nice and kind he was in the ways of a brother, pushed me inside the toilet of his house and locked the door, then thrust his fingers forcefully between my legs. It hurt so much I think I stopped breathing for about three seconds, before frantically banging on the door to alert my big sister. There was some hushed and quiet talk between my Mother and his Mother and then within a few months he moved house.

Then at aged nine, I remember vividly how a boy of sixteen forced me to feel the skin on his penis on a freezing cold winter evening, when a group of us had stayed out longer than we should have, beneath a late December sky, on an old bit of waste land next to the prefabs where sometimes torn out pages of pornography magazines lay on the ground. I recoiled, my heart jumping in my chest when he placed my hand on to his hard warm flesh and made noises like he was asthmatic or something and then deposited a warm milky substance all over my small freezing cold hand. I sat for a time, feeling like I wasn't really there.

I momentarily slipped out of my body as I had done many times before and entered that familiar peaceful place in my mind, but only for a short time, as always, for when I stepped back, the memory revisited vividly. The mists of time would gradually dilute any shame I had felt, I would eventually forget. Funny how life has a tendency to do that, to the point of something becoming non-existent; even though it had once hurt so deeply, it becomes a void within the consciousness, despite the body still revealing the scars even as the years unfold.

Robert and I did sex many times after that first time. He seemed to enjoy it and I would never let on that I thought it was utterly horrible. We had done most things together and been to lovely places that I hadn't even known had existed, even though they were only a short distance outside of our town. Like the strikingly beautiful Northumberland moors, wild and desolate, where the wind blew like a weeping violin to the dances of Fairy Kings and Queens. The unperturbed Ghosts looking out from the Castles that edged the steep and lofty cliffs, their beautiful forms reflected in the grey waters of the sea beneath. They eked out their existence in lonely isolation and I felt deeply for their tortured souls. I saw them, and sometimes I'm sure they saw me.

Mine and Robert's relationship was deepening, though he would never get to know anything of my courtship with the Spirit World. It was bad enough that he had to contend with my uncontrollable emotional outbursts that ruined the best of days. I could still count on Bernadette to be the calm voice of reason. She had an almost therapeutic effect on me at times, balancing the high levels of stress I seemed to constantly experience, which had become 'normal' for me. I looked in to the oval shaped mirror I sat holding, and surveyed from behind Bernadette's lacquered eye lids and sensuous lips, as she was busy getting ready for a special date. I was in such a quandary I barely knew how to explain; nobody would understand, I indulged myself emotionally.

"How can I possibly invite Robert back to mine, Bernadette?" I asked her, as I back-combed my hair in to a perfect stork's nest, watching her in the mirror as she writhed into her skin tight pencil skirt and bat-winged top.

I was at last beginning to afford a few of the latest fashions on my small YTS wage as a Solicitor's Receptionist, but nothing was ever quite like the creations Bernadette's Mother still made.

"I mean it's not as if he will ever have seen anything like my house before," I carried on. "I mean they're Conservative! His Dad was a GP for God's sake!"

Bernadette clicked her tongue disapprovingly by my blasphemous outburst. Unlike me, she still attended Church every Sunday.

Sucking in her belly to pinch the top button in to the buttonhole, she checked me sharply.

"I happen to like your Dad these days, Diane!" she said. "You've even said yourself he's changed."

I shrugged. She was right up to a point, I admitted. His last Court case laid out in no uncertain terms exactly what the penalty would be if he chose to get locked up again for kicking in a Policeman, or smashing up the bar at closing time when he was refused one last pint of 'Newcastle Brown Ale'. That had been almost a year ago now. After that he threw in the towel and quit drinking. He worked like a Trojan running at least two Council refuse sites, sometimes going out at dawn and not returning again until dusk; but old habits die hard and folk lore amongst the town's people where we lived, even harder. Sometimes grown men would come knocking on our door in the middle of the night asking him for a fight; just to take over his title, though I never really understood what that was about. I've seen me many a time run barefoot in to our street and clobber them over the head with one of my stilettos until my Dad told me to get back inside the house. I was protective of him, though God knows why, as he certainly didn't need my protection.

"No," I continued, resisting Bernadette's disapproving look. "Robert is never going to be on the receiving end of the she-nanigans that go on in our house!" Of that I was quite adamant.

I was very intrepid about taking anyone back, least of all Robert and not just because of Dad's unpredictable outbursts but also the inside of our house, which no matter how often it was cleaned, to me, would always resemble something out of 'Cath-erine Cookson's' cottages; grimy and depressing. Mam never knew what he would bring home next; there were boxes and boxes of things piled up in the dining room, making it impossible to get in. Sometimes he brought home ex-shop goods, chocolates and biscuits which had been dumped on the tip because they were soiled or slightly fire damaged or had reached their sell by date. Sometimes he would carry in ex-display furniture which had a slight discoloring from being in the shop window. Once he even brought home a drinks 'Bar', apparently because it was 'fashionable' he told us exuberantly, even though clearly it was the very unfashionable type, with the mock quilted front and teak interior and never had anything to drink in it except a drop of his home-made Ginger Ale at Christmas; stuff which took the lining off your gullet on the way down.

I was proud and full of ego and I wasn't letting Robert have anything to do with it; but fate would dictate that I would have very little choice in the matter and less than a week later he turned up unexpectedly, unannounced in the middle of my cleaning out one of the many fish tanks we had in our living room. I had spent the day cleaning and tidying but nothing I seemed to do would improve the appearance. I had begged Mam to let me put the Bar in the garden out of sight, under a pile of tarpaulin and old mattresses. After all it was utterly useless, I pined; clearly the room would look a little smarter without that hideous thing. Her look was one of humor and annoyance. She would do anything to avoid another argument with Dad and I didn't blame her because even a small insignificant remark could turn in to a full blown fight.

I felt like a traitor to her cause. I would catch her occasionally glancing at me as I balanced on one leg, on the chair, to reach up and hook the curtain back over the curtain-wire and clean the tops of the windows. I knew how proud she was as a person and I questioned how I could be so shallow. After all she had to live there, so surely she wanted more than this too?

My sisters were, by now, all married with homes of their own and I was the last, apart from my youngest brother John, who'd dropped out of School seemingly without the consent of the 'Education Authorities', who after several valiant attempts to pass 'Court Orders' to Dad over the door step, gave up. Not surprisingly, after a tall smart gentleman was chased all the way down the street back to his car where he just about made it in time or I daren't imagine what might have happened to him. Clearly he was no match for the force of nature such as my Dad was. It was a great pity however, that John had fallen out of the education system. He became more isolated as time went on, often spending whole days reading academic books. He had an amazing ability to retain information and History in particular was his passion.

I couldn't remember any of my sisters sharing their feelings of shame about the disarray of our house in the past and they had all seemingly passed the approval from their boyfriends, who had whisked them down the aisle in ceremonious style. I convinced myself that I was just being egotistical, as even our Thomas had popped the question to my friend Lilly and she had accepted and she lived in one of the posh houses on the newly built Leach estate with lovely summer houses built on to the back of them and big gardens that over looked the woods. Why would Robert care where I lived anyway? I listened to myself rant. I was just being over sensitive.

Perhaps it was just discontentment that I felt living in such disarray but whatever it was, I was becoming increasingly intolerant generally and wished for what others had. My friends all had smart houses and at least they did normal family things.

Mine just warred over petty things; everything from politics to burnt crust on a pie, and in particular 'money', or the lack of it. That relentless topic of conversation was repeated a million times over. Night after night, all we got was the 'evils of money' or 'money is hard to come by' and 'people will stab you in the back for it'. On and on I heard it. 'Never enough money '. The same old story, day after day, I'd had enough of listening. After hearing my Dad arguing one day, I jumped out of my seat and shouted at him to 'Shut up!' I couldn't stand it any longer and as I fled past him, I punched him neatly and squarely on his ear. I felt it was hard, it certainly hurt my knuckle so it must have hurt him. I was momentarily stunned before grabbing my coat and fleeing out of the back door, fearing that he might come after me. Of course, naturally, being my Dad, he was most impressed by that 'right upper cut' as he called it later.

"Dinky, look," he pointed to his purplish red swollen ear. "Helluva good punch, Dinky," he joked and family events would countless times see that story regurgitated. Long after it was firmly engraved on everyone's memory, there would always be one final tale to tell.

As hard as I tried, it was futile. Cleaning was impossible as we couldn't even use nice smelling disinfectant because Dad had an aversion to smells and flowers, especially in vases on window sills or scented candles or even soaps for that matter. Even the lovely, soft-scented ones that left a lingering smell and even basic brands of washing-up liquid had to have very little fragrance, otherwise he erupted in anger. He would swear he could taste it in his food, the sickly smell of flowers, he would say. These sensory issues and aversions he had, I knew little about then, but they would eventually make sense in time and in my work with people with Autism and Asperger's Syndrome.

Our living room was crammed with tanks containing Piranhas and Terrapins and other marine-type creatures so that the only thing you could smell upon going in was warm, putrid fish poo. I used to make jokes with my friends that we had a menagerie but when I look back we really did. There were six cats, a dog, a Canary, sea creatures of varying ferociousness which roamed the floor at night with razor sharp teeth. We had ferrets and even a goat, which was kept in our garden shed until the local authorities made my Dad give her to a local farm.

The day Robert showed up unannounced, the panic I felt when his lovely car pulled up outside our gate unexpectedly, I'll never forget. I had just plopped the fan-tailed Gold-fish back in to their lovely clean tank and dashed to get the door; but no sooner had I opened it to let him in when I heard the loud engine of Dad's van roar to a halt in the back lane. I must've turned a shade of grey as Robert squeezed me to him and told me not to worry. Oh, he wouldn't say that if he knew, I panicked, as I rushed him past the kitchen into the living room and out of Dad's sight. I would gauge Dad's mood first before deciding whether or not to introduce Robert and possibly run the risk of him finishing with me for good. My mind went into a sort of military operation mode; I remember thinking, maybe if we were quick we could escape through the garden out of Dad's sight and I could run him round the front, up the back street and straight in to his car before anyone even noticed he was there!

But as it happened Dad was in a positively wonderful mood. The tip where he still worked had received a delivery container of copper wire just before he had set off home, which he announced was worth a small fortune. I was confident that luck was raining down on us that day, for as complementary and generous as my Dad could be, he was equally moody and foul-mouthed. Thankfully for me, he liked Robert and instantly charmed his way in to my boyfriend's heart.

Yet despite its positive beginnings, my entrance into romantic love was paved with pot-holes and unexploded ordinances; which weekly Robert and I trod on with devastating consequences. Heated arguments were frequent and it appeared no matter how hard he reassured me that he loved me, I was beset with jealousy and insecurity which marred any hope of a future together. My diaries which had once been filled with light-hearted dreams and aspirations were now half attempts to indulge my sorrow and satisfy my misery and I seemed unable to muster feelings of positivity of any kind.

I wondered where I'd gone wrong and how I'd gotten so lost as my diary reflected this deep-seated sadness.

*'City Wolves cry out against the noise, Oh let my Spirit be Free!'*

I looked at the strewn of writing etched on the page of my now tatty diary.

*"Naught!' came the mighty reply. "Might ye cease to wail for in thy own creation did ye alone build thy own prison cell."*

*'But my World has taken from me my Soul, in emptiness now do I carry this Heart'*

Tears had smudged some of my writing, making it quite difficult to read.

*'How can I look to a future so devoid of all that I deem worthy?*
*Where to look for Strength and Protection and for Solace?*

*When all is quiet in the night, who will shine the light of Faith*
*into my Dreams? To nurture my Desires and shape all the days*
*to come?'*

*Rain fell on to outstretched palms and the voice answered in*
*the Silence.*

*'I watch ore' ever with calm patience and the eyes of the World*
*lower from my gaze and I say unto you. Let tomorrow take care*
*of itself. For today, free thyself from all this that you fear and only*
*then will you know, who and what you are. Only then will you see*
*that the light shining in thy dreams is of thine own making. For*
*ye' alone can light the flame of thy existence'*

I had written speedily, exhausted almost by the desperation
to move the words on paper as fast as they came in to my head.
I didn't know then, that my spirit had long awakened to something that had been a part of me since birth. I was at last coming
to acknowledge, if only in part, that I was an instrument for a
higher voice of reason, of this I have no doubt in my mind. I
turned the page, my mind trying to understand.

*'I am a significant part of life',* I had written.

*'Stored within the Universal-Mind. I do not see myself clearly*
*for the density of matter of which I am made. How could anything*
*so weighty ever fly? How could I possibly conceive of the notion of*
*an Eternal life when I am effervescent by thick walls of Ego? Even*
*though light-colour transmits from the cages of my body, I am still*
*rooted in the soil of the material world'*

I surveyed the scrawled writing, little resembling my own
neat hand, which I couldn't make much sense of and wondered
if I was depressed. Yes, I thought, perhaps that was it, after all
how can you lose your soul? I was only eighteen! What was I

doing even contemplating it? I had begun to drink alcohol to dull the sense of feelings of despair. It never even occurred to me, that perhaps I was 'normal', all things considered. I had found a way of escaping with alcohol and I liked it, though it has never particularly liked me.

The sweet path of young love ended abruptly, sometime amidst the glorious eighties, tearfully and passionately and with all the intensity of a TV Soap drama. Naturally I was devastated. Robert and I had been together for nearly two years and almost inseparable during that time, even though for the latter half, we had argued almost weekly. Mostly because of my insatiable jealousy, that made 'loving me difficult', as Robert had often told me. Especially towards the end; and despite all my best efforts, I simply couldn't change the record, which I repeatedly listened to internally, the drumming of negative self-effacing dialogue which rejoiced seeing me in pain.

For Robert, my heart, I conceded, actually did break. I mourned like someone I loved had just died and after weeks of inconsolable distress, with Mam telling me constantly that I would get over him, eventually, one morning I awoke with a renewed purpose and I vowed that I would not be so foolish in love as to spoil things. The next time round, if a next time came around, that was; which of course it did, probably far too quickly on reflection, shortly after my last tearful goodbye with Robert.

I donned my stilettos with indignation, reached for my clutch bag and stepped out with a purpose and rebellion that was to become my companion. I would stop living in the place of suffering and guilt. I would choose not to surrender to the emotional convulsions that threatened me constantly and consequently because of this decision, I am sure 'Love' whatever love was, called me to its side.

Tony Pritchard was the gift I believe Spirit gave me in which to uplift my heart and put me back on to the path of self-belief, though sadly if only briefly. He was seven years older than me and carried a maturity way beyond his twenty five years; as though he might even have been born with this wisdom. He was a Royal Naval Sailor, which may well have attributed to him being so self-assured and confident, having travelled all over the world and experienced so much of life, which I found undeniably attractive.

With his flecked blonde-on-ginger hair and open honesty that radiated from his light, sea-blue eyes, there was something about him which set him apart from the rest. Perhaps it was his protectiveness that I liked, the way in which he laughed off my suspicions and seriousness and had a way of looking at the world which just filled me with wonder. I longed to go to the places he described, which I could see in my mind's eye. I basked in his glorious simplicity; simplicity that sadly I was always going to spoil, given what I now know was a recurrent feature in my relationships, which no matter how hard anyone tried to reassure me that they loved me, I could not accept. As though I pressed an erase button every time I heard those three words. I felt unlovable and was desperately insecure with it.

Tony's job took him away for months on end and his absence only fueled my suspicions. My friends all joked that a 'Sailor had a girl in every Port' and though I didn't really believe he could be unfaithful, by his very nature, he was too honest if anything, the thought still wormed it's way deep in to my subconscious.

His phone calls were always punctual, as promised, whenever he was ashore, with his light-hearted way of somersaulting my heart. He would ask about my family, how everyone was and then he would tell me how much he missed me and loved me. He would chatter about things he had done, and the amazing places around the world where his ship docked. I listened intently, imagining the sights and sounds he described.

"I'll bring you back something from every country I visit Diane, I promise," he said, his soft southern accent quiet and gentle. Silence stole my words. Like a sharp wind that takes your breath away. "You still there love? Diane, love?" he whispered.

I wanted to say I love you back. I wanted to tell him, reassure him that I was also thinking about him and longed for him to come back, because that's how I truly felt, but instead I told him coldly, "It's useless holding on to me."

I heard myself say as if a twin had taken hold of my vocal cords, "You would be better off bedding some girl in one of the many places you visit."

My heart ached with every word, a malevolent painful stabbing sensation right in to my breast bone. I knew it was hurting him, but I just couldn't stop.

"There's no-one like you to me, love." Tony's voice was a hushed reassuring whisper, cracking with emotion.

I hated myself deeply for the pain I caused when all I wanted to say was 'I love you': those three little words, which I found impossible to say, as though I was programmed to respond with negativity in order to protect myself. Of course, I didn't realize then, that's exactly what I was doing, yet thoughts of comprehension don't come whilst the Schemas are being played out ritually, time and time again. It was only after years of deep reflection and therapy that I understood it a little more clearly, and even then the most natural response was one of negativity first, as though a groove in a dirt track forged out by endless cars would always take the driver down that road naturally, unless he consciously veered off in another direction.

I replaced the receiver of the telephone and headed out in to the garden, feelings of complete overwhelming sadness consumed every part of me; which is difficult to find words to express how immobilizing such an emotion feels like, made worse when it seems if it is self-induced, perpetuated by nothing but spitefulness, or that's what I believed it to be then.

Autumn had spread her orange and gold cloak upon the trees, and a cool breeze moved the leaves about on the ground in patterns. I felt exiled and lonely. Dad was busy in the shed, banging and clattering as he moved stuff around and Mam was sitting by the open fire in her chair, watching early evening telly, with John reading quietly near her. The house, I realized was quiet, which it seemed it had become more of late, as though a spell had been lifted and Mam and Dad were able to speak without needing to fight with each other. I sighed at the incomprehensible reality of things.

The light of the sun was soothing, casting a warm glow over everything. I would walk off this somber mood, I remember thinking and see how far I could get before the sun went down. I walked over the fields, past Roly-Poly Hill, watching cars in the distance, noticing every tree that was familiar. I fell in to a state of pleasurable participatory intimacy, seeing a couple of well-fed Mallards making their way to the edge of the stream. I followed a footpath down and stood with my feet almost touching the steel-blue water, whilst the fading sun vanished beneath a grey, dappled cloud. I felt I could easily have been the last soul on earth. Long Forge woods was uninviting in the dusk and for the first time, it felt that I might even be suffocated by the trees, with their long trailing fingers. My heart cracked open and I started to cry softly. I don't know how long for.

I was cold and unprepared for the long walk home without a warm coat and I knew that by the time I returned it would be pitch black and I didn't relish that walk across the fields. I emptied my mind, absorbed only by the stillness and trill of the birds. I knew I had to muster the strength within myself to fight the consuming battle of conscience still raging on in my mind. It's amazing how strong the will is over the mind, which will lure you back to feelings of self-defeat if you allow it to. In the quiet, the same strong, 'living energy' told me that everything was going to be alright. Later, as I stepped across the doorway, I caught a glimpse of myself in the passage-way mirror and as I walked back in to the house, I had a rosy glow on my cheeks and a lighter halo above me.

Tony came home after several more weeks, which I filled with work and seeing friends. On the afternoon he came back, I donned my most fantastic red dress and high heeled boots. I painted on far too much make up but I admired myself appreciatively in the bathroom mirror. Dad made me laugh.

"Dinky," he said stopping on the landing before going down stairs.

"How long is it ye've been in that bathroom, two hours or summit? I don't know but yer never seem to look any different!" he said.

"Charming" I said, as I craned my neck to see Tony's posh hire car pull up outside the house, my heart starting to beat like a freight train.

"Dad," I said firmly. "Listen, Tony's here and I don't want you embarrassing me or anything like that!" Stupid me, I thought, rushing downstairs, he's bound to now I've said it.

Oh, how my Mam loved Tony. She told me over tea that day, smiling warmly she said if she could've picked anyone in the world for me, she would've picked him. He was already in the kitchen offloading arms full of presents for me and the family on to the kitchen table and when he saw me his face lit up.

"You look beautiful, love." He kissed me softly, "Lady in Red."

As promised, he made me open a present from all the different countries he had visited. He knew I loved boxes and there was a gorgeous dark oak wooden box inlaid with Mother of Pearl and coral from Turkey and little soap stone elephants which he told me were lucky, from Morocco; beautiful objects from all parts of the Mediterranean. I felt unbelievably spoiled and when Mam said later that I would never find anyone in the world who loved me like he did, I understood why.

I wanted us to make love not just have sex, like times before. I imagined it to be the way I read about in 'Mills and Boons', heart throbbing, amazing love making, I couldn't wait to make it up to him for the horrible way I had behaved.

"I've got a surprise for you," he said taking a leaflet out of his coat pocket and showing it to me, "a beautiful old-fashioned lodge on Lake Windermere. You better pack an overnight bag because that's where we're headed."

Wave on wave of warm security bathed through me. My head was slightly intoxicated with wine and with fingers entwined, Tony and I rolled on to the huge king-size bed of our hotel room, with the warm lights from the lake creating the feeling of candlelight. We kissed for so long, my whole being felt as if I could have glided up to the sky, I felt so wanted and loved. All thoughts left me, as I immersed myself in this beautiful sacred expression of love. I could've done it forever, I needed nothing more. Or so I thought.

As advent of that year drew in for both of us, as the pines were ignited with bright fairy-lights of red and gold holly berries glistening in the golden winter sunlight, a hushed mood stirred within me, withdrawing me in to the silence. It seemed the endlessly long days of waiting for Tony's return had turned me in to a negative person, oscillating somewhere between hopeful anticipation and the dismissive sneer of rejection. I hardly knew how things could've gone so badly wrong. I turned to my diary for peace and wrote.

*'I am element, I am water and in the lull of calm winds, I am Ethereal,*

*In the stark shadows, I am Light.*

*My Spirit is composite of integrated colours, vibrating in a steady density, shifting and changing and forever emanating.*

*I am the cool spring that flows down blue-bell Mountain.*

*I am the Indian Spirit forever free.*

*As the cloud creates another unearthly formation, I am.*

*For every moment as it lifts the veil of emotion and*

*In it wells some vein of Truth, I recognize that I am All and in All do I find expression of being.*

*There is no fixation on growth as it spirals and flows out in all Directions, like seeds scattered by the wind.*

*I am the Seasons,*

*I live in the Caverns within the Oceans,*

*I find flight in the Forests as Bird and Beast and in the Heavens I ascend as terrestrial within the Cosmos.*

*I am the Expansion of Spirit HERE and NOW and unto ETERNITY. I AM'*

I attempted to hold the diary I had written so freely in only yesterday, the words thick, black and stark on a white page. I felt like I wanted to be sick but I didn't dare move for fear I would throw up. I had lain for several hours drifting in and out of sleep, seeing the room spin above me; allowing the silence to filter the conversations going round and round in my mind, waiting for a lull in the pounding headache so I could attempt to get up.

Behind closed eye lids I could still see Tony's ashen face, forlorn and crumpled as if he had aged a decade in an hour; searching my eyes for a glimpse of remorse.

"Why Diane?" he pleaded, "I thought you loved me?"

How could I tell him that my infidelity had nothing whatsoever to do with me not loving him; how could I explain that in my mind you could love someone yet still hurt them? Adore them yet still betray them? Cling to some part of you that felt whole, all the while feeling so utterly in pieces; needing to feel loved and wanted in order to fill a vacuum of empty space within? None of it made any sense any more. I had pushed Tony so far away as to make it impossible for us to ever come back together again. The trust was broken and at that moment I realized that despite the tenacity of the Spirit to overcome adversity, the Mind/Body can become trapped in an inescapable vault of pain of which the key to unlock it, is deeply hidden.

Just as the Summer had brought the refreshing beginnings of new love, Winter, with all its promises from Saints and Angels declaring their message of hope, instead, brought only shadows into the corners of my life which were already in darkness. If only to die laughing at the irony.

# Chapter Four

## *Flowers of Spirit*

"Hey there!" A familiar voice startled me as I was hurrying into a shop doorway to avoid the heavy rain.

"My God!" I could hardly believe my eyes. "Bernadette!"

It was easily two years since I had seen her, last time being at her leaving party before going to University in Edinburgh. We hugged and chatted as if there wasn't a second to lose. I poured out my stories and she listened with that same old seriousness which made the weight on my shoulders feel a little lighter.

"Why not go out tonight eh? Let's sod it! A few drinks in town and a good ole' dance." Bernadette's face beamed.

I couldn't help but think how well and happy she looked. Her sun kissed hair a shade lighter, she almost had an aura of love about her. She took a picture from out of her purse, as if reading my mind and placed it in to my hand. Blue eyes shone out from the face of the man in the photograph, identical to hers in their expression of love. He was a lovely looking guy, I wistfully smiled.

"Oh Diane, I am so happy!" she continued. "He's asked me to move in with him already!" She giggled as if the idea was ludicrous, "We've only been seeing each other a few months!"

I laughed with her, intoxicated by her enthusiasm. I didn't want to dampen Bernadette's happiness by telling her about the misery that I felt my life had become. I wanted to bask gloriously in the light that she emanated and within minutes of being in her company I felt I had been whisked back to our girly Youth Club days, as we chatted endlessly about the silly and ridiculous larking about we got up to; it was refreshing, I felt young.

Later that evening, I spotted her waiting at the bus stop, waving her umbrella, head to toe in mauve and purple, with her skimpy top and skin tight jeans showing off every curve of her ample frame. I couldn't help smiling to myself. Bernadette, with her refreshing self-confidence, beaming like a little girl, unscarred by life, she could have easily still been fourteen, standing there bearing no concern for the young men walking past, their eyes firmly feasting on her large bosoms.

She twirled me around excitedly.

"Girl you look fantastic!" she complimented, eyeing my fairly fashionable but a little shy and retiring by comparison outfit. I was curvy in a modest way. I wore black and white as if it was compulsory but I felt good in high court shoes and heavy makeup, thick black eyeliner. It's amazing what a disguise can do for the flagging spirit.

As usual, of course, I was impressed by the attention I got from a few good looking boys who gave me ample admiration and ordered me several cocktails. It was an easy way to loosen up and forget the crap. I provocatively danced, moving deliberately to attract attention, something which I loved doing, suspended in drama of being a sort of 'Gypsy Queen' dancing around a fire with bells on her toes, enticing villains to chance their fate. Of course, Bernadette being Bernadette stole the limelight every time with her moves to hits such as 'Take my breath away' by 'Berlin' and her mesmerizing breast action which had all heads following them in trance-like state. Like a snake charmer, she never failed. We laughed and giggled and danced like ten year olds, just stopping for breath and another round of drinks.

With my head still light and heady I wrote slowly the next day.

*'Dear diary, my thoughts have been all over the place of late, in fact I have half wondered if I might even be going mad. Is it possible to be this confused yet still think that somehow you're where you're meant to be? Do you think insanity is a 'conscious state' that you're aware of? If it is, then I am most definitely crazy!*

*Yesterday when Bernadette and I were out in Newcastle I met a boy (I know …another)… anyway, I noticed someone's back resting against mine as we were sat at the bar. At first I thought it was just us being squashed because the Pub was really busy, but after a little while I realized that it wasn't that at all, we were both actually leaning up against one another. We sort of turned around at the same time and started laughing.*

*Oh diary, he was gorgeous in a rugged sort of a way. He reminded me of 'George Michael' from 'Wham' with streaked blonde hair and oh so trendy clothes! I told him straight away that I thought he looked nice (laugh) and he said that he thought I looked like an Angel (can you believe! Me an Angel?!). Anyway, we're meeting again tonight!*

*I know I'm out of control and I should really be stopping in and getting over Tony, but the thing is diary, I don't want to think about it... I just want to let go and see what happens... After all, what've I got to lose!?'*

Perhaps, if I'd stopped at that point in time, to consider the events that had led me to that place, I would have understood how my emotions had taken more than a little battering from an endless struggle in a hope to experience peace. I might have been more sympathetic to the hurting child within who valiantly appeared to lead me along dead ends in her quest to find love. The values and judgments that I'd placed on myself were understandably negative given how my family life was so critical and self-depreciating. These values, nevertheless took up prime residency within my psyche, and undoubtedly altered my aspirations, my thoughts and indeed the very course of my life. However, I neither decry nor regret the family I was born in to, without them I may never have deepened my spiritual faith but I was a very long way from realizing it then.

My bus pulled in to Newcastle, Worswick Street Station, just as Mike was turning the corner and as a smattering of rain was falling. I remember that he was striding confidently with one hand in his pocket and the other carrying a black umbrella. He was wearing a pale pink shirt over a white t-shirt and light denim jeans and because the bus was full, I had time to view him from the upper deck before getting off. He looked exactly as I remembered from the evening before, perhaps slightly taller than I thought, but definitely attractive from what I could see. I felt a little self-conscious, nervous even, as I alighted the bus and sucked in my tummy to give me a more slim-line look.

For days I had been comfort eating and my normal size 10 figure was rapidly becoming a size 12 and furthermore, I had no money in which to buy new clothes, so my old stuff just had to do. It didn't appear to matter at all, as you'd think a Super Model had just stepped out in front of him the way his eyes lit up when he saw me. The word 'genuine' came to my mind at once. I linked his arm immediately, partly because I was sharing his umbrella but also because it felt so comfortable, as though we had been mates for years. From the word go, Mike and I had an easy sort of a connection when we were together, which made it easier for us to slip in to something cozy which didn't necessarily spell out relationship.

He was the sort of person who chatted openly and liked to ask lots of questions which dissolved any inhibitions I had about my past. In fact he seemed to almost counsel me on occasions, when I felt myself naturally wanting to run. I trusted and liked him. He was fun and kind, with a good sense of humor which we seemed to share. He played in a band and sometimes, when he played guitar quietly to me, he looked directly into my eyes. It made my heart skip a beat.

Within weeks I was introduced to his family and I felt an affinity with his Mother instantly. Theirs was a relaxed middle-class suburban home, with objects of taste from their many travels in Spain and their family who lived there. Early on in our friendship I was welcomed, encouraged even, to stay at Mike's home, which he shared with his Mother and two brothers and I jumped at the opportunity whenever I could.

You'd be forgiven for thinking that throughout this time, I was able to tolerate my own family life a little easier, because of the times I spent at Mikes, however, if anything, I was finding it harder and harder to bear. Now that my sisters and brother had left, I felt imprisoned within my own silence. Violent arguments still erupted when Dad became frustrated, usually because someone had threatened him on his tip and he was consumed with anger and talked relentlessly about the past and his days spent in Borstal and solitary confinement.

John, by this time, had also become extremely argumentative and sometimes the pair of them would shout for up to two hours without let up. Whenever I was at home it felt that I regressed and the same recurring dreams and haunting insecurities would return. I'd all but stopped writing entries in my diary, mostly because I was too tired after I'd finished work and instead I began jotting down thoughts as they came to me instead.

Seven weeks after our first meeting, though it was quick, Mike and I decided to try and find a small place of our own, as our travelling to see each other was costing us a lot of money. Mike was a practical person and the idea of saving money was sensible, after all we were seeing each other every other day. For me it was the chance to get away from the upsets of everyday life. In some ways, having more space in the bedroom at home was refreshing after finally getting to own a wardrobe now that my sisters had left and I'd even painted the walls a cheerful lemon colour, yet none of this meant anything, when the heated arguments began and Dad's established patterns of behavior resulted in the same old unbearable situation of him becoming so angry as to completely lose control. After years of it and though possible to desensitize to his inexhaustible rants and threats of violence, in truth, I never got used to seeing Mam's frustration and upset and sadly, it was something I would never be able to prevent.

Moving in with Mike seemed a logical thing to do at the time, even though we didn't have a bean or a single stick of furniture between us. The frustrations which had led me to leave home and its eventual fulfilment, projected me in to a realm of experience for which I had no preparation. There was no way of knowing then, I was about to slide in to the darkest place I had ever experienced.

On the eve of signing the lease agreement for the tenancy, I wrote;

'Lauded art thou who claims to know thine own self,
Halted in this mortal kingdom.
Dost thou see shape, form and image?
What then is conjured within the depths of thy mind?
Dost thou deny the existence of an eternal realm?
If thou dost choose to contemplate such mysteries, might
Thy heart sing in eternity with those who have passed
In to the borderlands between worlds, to exist in harmony

*And peace with their higher spiritual self.*
*Listen in the stillness, when the eyes of the world sleeps.*
*For then, the chorus of Angels ring out their song.*
*To call thee to rejoice!*
*And to live!'*

I had no idea when I wrote that, how portentous these words were going to be.

The flat we took in haste, was little more than squalor in reality. In fact, it had stood empty for months, before becoming home to squatters, who used it as a place to take drugs, as the Landlord gleefully told us whilst signing the Lease Agreement. The place stank of acrid tom-cat pee and the heavily patterned carpets reeked of it and stuck to the bottom of your shoes as you walked. Nicotine yellow-coloured wood-chip paper lined every wall, most of which was peeling off, revealing graffiti underneath, I wondered how the Landlord dared to confess to owning it, it was a shamble. Still, I thought to myself, Mike and I will have it pulled round in no time.

Unfortunately, however, Mike's job had ended, because of his Company laying people off and though he was still doing gigs with his Band, my pittance of a salary as a Solicitor's receptionist was nowhere near enough to pay the bills and buy things to improve the flat. We could barely afford to eat let alone buy cheap magnolia paint and most of the things we had were borrowed from Mike's Mother. We had an old double mattress as a make-shift sofa which also doubled up as a bed. My sisters donated dishes, cutlery and pans, we lifted the carpets and scrubbed the floorboards and cleaned every square inch of the place and yet within a few weeks we knew it was futile, we simply couldn't afford it. Devastatingly, we realized, that we had no alternative but to move back to our parents. Mike and I had become very close, it felt so right living together and even though we couldn't afford to do anything or go anywhere, we were happy and things were good between us.

I gathered my few possessions together, which fitted in to a hold-all and sat looking around the room. Mike had already left, reassuring me before he did, that if I needed to, I could easily go and stay with his family. We had made an arrangement to call each other later. I counted the coins in my purse and realized that I didn't have enough to take the bus. Reluctantly, I would have to walk the couple of miles to get home, but luckily, at least it wasn't raining, I thought, as I closed the door of the flat behind me.

As I walked the quiet road over the footbridge past the old disused railway station, I couldn't identify the feeling I had inside. It was a nervous kind of feeling, the sort which leaves you shaking slightly, quivering almost with anxiety. I felt an unholy alliance to the cynical voice within, reminding me that I had failed again, telling me how loathed and utterly hopeless I'd become.

By the time I reached Mam and Dads I was a quivering wreck and I just about fell in to Mam's arms, crying. I felt so tired from the walk and even the mug of tea she made me, felt heavy. Within ten minutes of me walking in, Dad appeared at the doorway I knew instantly he was in a bad mood.

"Ya cannot come back, Dinky. I've made that bedroom into a boxing gym for John now. Ye've made ya bed, you'll have to lie in it."

I looked to Mam pleadingly, surely she would have the final word. She looked at me, her expression said a thousand words which I had read as 'hopeless' on her face many times.

"I can't go back, Mam," I said between sobs. "Mike and I haven't enough money to pay the rent this month and anyway the place needs condemned. It's damp and the roofs letting in."

"Whey man, that's nothing!" Dad shouted and laughed. "A bit of damp! Bloody hell if that's all that was wrong with our house when you were bairns' we'd have been happy." he said scathingly.

"We haven't got any money," I began. "Do you not see?" I broke down in tears.

"Listen!" Dad thumped his fist on the kitchen bench, "That's not my problem Dinky, yer'l just have to tell that bloke he'll get his rent next month."

Mam stubbed her cigarette out on the ashtray, "Stop tonight," she said, "You and Mike will sort it out tomorrow."

Dad began to laugh. "Whey that's it, like, Dinky. Ye've moved out. Ya cannot just say I want to come back, it doesn't work like that. Johns got his gym now."

"Stop tonight," Mam said again soothingly and she began to say something else but I didn't hear. I couldn't take in anything that was being said. As if time had slowed down, I slowly picked up my hold-all and numbly walked out the front door.

In a complete daze I walked the two miles back down the old road, as dark was settling in, diminishing the sky of the last few chinks of daylight. Tiny sparrows chirped in the hedgerow and because it was a minor road and not well lit, I stumbled several times, dropping my hold-all on the ground. At some point I sat down on the side of the road, feeling too exhausted to keep going.

"What do I do?" I repeated out loud, over and over again, begging for an answer, listening for some sympathy of my heart to tell me that all would be alright and that I could get through it.

I looked over the expanse of land like a colossal sleeping giant and I wished in that moment that it would swallow me up. I had never felt more alone. If things hadn't happened, words came unbidden in my mind, events that had irrevocably redirected my life, through circumstances of my own making and others out of my control, would I still have found myself here?

Realizing that all of life's roads had been leading me to this place, I suddenly found myself crying again. I can't remember walking the rest of the way back to the flat. My head felt numb and hollow. I turned the key in the front door and switched on the light only it didn't go on. I'd forgotten, the payment meter had run out and rather than replenishing it, Mike and I had decided it wasn't going to be worth it.

The street lights were bright enough so that I could just see what I was doing. I lit a large pillar candle and placed it on to the hearth, suddenly giving the room a glow, only it didn't glow; there was a gloominess which hung around like a somber incursion upon an oil painting and I felt like a ghost awaiting resurrection. Only I didn't want to exist. The delicate balance of reason had been outweighed by the condition of sickness within the mind and spirit.

I raked through the cupboard to find the box of Paracetemol tablets and a litre bottle of Vodka I hoped was still under the sink. If I was lucky, I thought, there would be enough of it to put me to sleep so that I wouldn't wake up. Yesterday's rain had caused more water to seep in to the kitchen, making foist on the walls smell damp. It made me want to wretch. I poured the Vodka into a half pint glass and gulped it down as if it was pop and pulled my coat around me as I huddled into the back of the mattress of our make-shift sofa. I was shivering from the cold but I didn't dare move either, scared now of the shadows that had transformed in the thick tangible darkness.

Tears welled in my eyes. I carefully popped all of the tablets out of the blister pack. There were sixteen of them, I held them in my hand and took another gulp of Vodka. There was a vacancy of thoughts, a sort of numbness from my heart-aching and from being so cold, then after a few moments I at once 'sensed' the dimension of Spirit draw close. The cavern of darkness suddenly became transformed by a vapor of light, like condensation appearing on glass, except it moved freely above me. I became aware of the familiar living energy of something or someone enter the room, which I wanted to rationalize away, only I couldn't. It was beyond the sense world we perceive with our intelligence.

Then a voice spoke in the darkness, it was barely audible, it whispered "Live." That was all, just "Live," but with calm authority that drew me from my despair. I couldn't deny I had heard it, it was abundant with mystery, yet familiar and loving. In that moment I was too numb to think. All I knew was that I was afraid. Afraid to live and yet too afraid to die. I felt that the decision wasn't mine to take. It was as if I was being made aware of the trouble it had taken for me to 'get here', at this place of desolation, and that I needed to accept without fault-finding or criticism and blame. That 'I' had at some point 'chosen' it all, and regardless of how it worked out, I would be allowed continuity of awareness and consciousness of the 'spiritual' or 'other side of life'.

It was an epiphany moment of clarity and purity of thought. I knew in my heart that whatever I was meant to do, it didn't involve me going back home, ever. The hurt I felt at my Dad's rejection was too great to bear. I yearned for Mike's embrace to ease the self-deprecation I was feeling but I also knew that I needed help from someone, whose skills would enable me to face the insurmountable challenges I knew lay ahead.

It was quarter past five in the morning, when I dialed Mike's home number from the phone box at the bottom of the street. I could barely press the numbers for the cold but within seconds he picked up as if he had been anticipating me calling and in between my sobs I heard him say "I'm on my way darlin', I'm coming back, I won't be long."

Over the next few weeks Mike and I accepted without questioning our situation, as though we had been destined to carry on, and though I was glad that I had someone who cared enough to want to stay, little by little I felt as if I was slipping in to a sort of melancholic reverie. I hated where we lived, in some ways it represented the house I had just left behind and with those thought brought back feelings of shame and anger. I never answered the door even when I knew it was friends and I became disassociated with family.

The evenings when Mike played in the band, I spent indulging in negative mental chatter. The world had completely changed and I didn't know where I fitted in anymore. We barely ate good food and then food went off with the damp in the kitchen and bread became moldy within days. We had a small, two-bar gas-fire which we couldn't afford to use and it wasn't powerful enough to heat the rooms. Therefore when Mike wasn't playing guitar in the evenings, we spent time mostly in bed keeping warm.

The odd occasion when we went out together, I ended up getting too drunk and regrettably, one such evening ended up with me being arrested for getting in to a fight with a bar-maid. It was a mistake which I sorely regretted, one that resulted in me getting a criminal record. Mike, however, was incredibly supportive throughout it all. He battled to uplift me, even when he must've been struggling with his own inner worries and anxieties.

March's shrill winds howled and ice had formed patterns on the insides of the windows and with each morning I found it harder and harder to get up. I felt unnaturally exhausted, and some days I could barely keep my eyes open and by mid-afternoon I was ready to sleep, which made my job in the Solicitor's almost impossible. I was irritable and clumsy and cried over the least little thing, I couldn't understand what was wrong with me.

I sat in the Doctor's waiting room listening for my name to be called, fidgeting with a glossy magazine, feeling a little apprehensive wondering what the Test Results would reveal. An article caught my eye about 'Meditation' and I recalled what Mr. Hammonds, the Consultant Psychiatrist had said the previous week when I broke down in tears in his office, exorcizing the hatred and sorrow I had been bottling up inside since I last went home.

''Not everything in life happens just the way we want it to,'' he viewed me seriously.

"Am I like him, Doctor?" I asked, almost afraid to hear his answer.

"You mean your Father?" He looked at me thoughtfully, "Do you think you're like your Father?" he repeated.

I thought of all the ways which I was. The uncontrolled anger which I felt possessed me at times of frustration. But was I cruel? I implored, surely I wasn't cruel like him?

Dr. Hammond's deep voice brought me back.

"Hurt, insecurity and pain cause people to act in ways at times they can't control and sometimes reflecting on those things with another person who isn't involved can help considerably. I don't see you being like your Father, Diane, at least not in the ways you fear. I think you just need to talk to someone who will listen."

He smiled reassuringly. It felt like healing balm had cleansed my soul, all at once I felt at ease. I think I had internalized those questions my whole life.

I heard my name being called by the Doctor's Receptionist and it snapped me back to reality. I clicked open the door of the Doctor's room. He had the kind of face that made you instantly smile, unreserved and gregarious, he welcomed me in to the chair.

"How long is it since you had a period?" he asked immediately.

I had to think. It was quite normal for me to have long gaps when I wouldn't have a period and taking the contraceptive pill meant that I could go months without seeing it.

"Two and a half months, maybe three," I calculated, wondering why he was asking. There was a slight pause, then leaning over his desk and peering over his glasses he said,

"That's because you're pregnant!"

I didn't notice the fog that had descended as I walked home, obscuring the lights from the cars and shop windows. I was in a sort of daze. When I reached the flat, I could barely see a hand in front of me to place the key in the lock but Mike opened the door with an expression of anticipation.

"We're going to have a baby," I blurted out instantly, the minute he opened the door. All I remember seeing was Mike's shocked expression and the blurred whitewashed walls of woodchip wall paper.

Despite the unknown of being pregnant and of all that it entailed, in that instant, I truly felt my heart break wide open. It was as if spirit had taken a torch and flooded a long corridor with bright light and for the first time in my whole life I felt there was a reason to be here, that every thought, act and choice created a ripple of consciousness which had affected all our lives. Mike reached out and held me lovingly.

"A baby," he whispered, several times.

We stood motionless for a long time, until I began to cry, I looked up at him, and his rich coffee brown eyes were full of tears too.

'*Each moment is golden, as it sends a spray of everlasting memories which*

*Are retained upon the threshold of time and space, where they remain forever*

*Like the first snows, pure.*

*And unto each and every moment, we gain insight anew and glean*

*Life's hidden mysteries.*

*Cherish each moment, for in each and every moment, lies*

*Unlimited opportunity*'

I held the piece of paper I had written on and wondered about the opportunities that lay ahead for us, now we had a new life to consider. I felt so afraid and yet at the same time, incredibly blessed.

## Chapter Five

# Fruits of Spirit

After the long spell of winter, finally we stepped over the threshold of our new flat, which was above a boarded-up bakery shop, a stone's throw away from where our old one had been. Once inside we viewed the patterned Axminster carpet as if it was made of gold threads, it was so thick and luxurious. My belly by now was enormous and Mike helped me climb the steep stairs of our new home, which was to be an interim transition place until we were housed by the local County Council Authority, which we were advised could take anything up to twelve months. After my second chest infection, within two months and us appealing to our local MP to fight on our behalf, we were finally given a confirmation from the Council, that the next available two bedroom house would be ours, in the meantime however, on the grounds of my depleting health, we were issued a Social Security grant by the government to put down as a deposit on a more suitable place to live.

By comparison, the new flat was like a mansion. It had a large lounge with high ceilings and alcoves at one side and wall lights either end of a red brick fire place. The walls were painted a garish green and a lurid, rich, heavily-patterned burgundy paper adorned the feature wall. Items of furniture were sparsely placed around the room, lost almost by its sheer dimensions, but I admired them appreciatively. They were a welcome sight after what we had just left, especially the large brown sofa which was a god-send after spending months sitting on our makeshift mattress.

Inside the kitchen, neat brown and cream cupboards lined the walls, complemented by light brown tiles and wood-effect bench tops. It really was quite posh, I thought, looking out of the large window which let in lots of light and overlooked a spacious yard beneath. In the bedroom, on the far side, was our new, unwrapped double bed, which Mike's Grandmother had kindly purchased for us, and on the other wall, was a rather formidable looking old fashioned mirrored teak wardrobe, with a dated electric fire, mounted on to the wall beside.

I shuddered mildly the first time I entered that room. There was a slight musky smell in there, which although wasn't horrible, it made me think of death somehow. It brought back memories of old Sid Spencer and that mossy smell of foist which accompanied him on the day his house got fumigated. I instantly disliked the formidable mirrored wardrobe. I had never liked mirrors facing you in a bedroom anyway and come to think of it, I had never liked peering into an old mirror full stop. The thought of looking at your reflection and seeing the appearance of someone else standing there fixated itself in my mind.

Mam's voice came to me as I looked at it.

"You and your vivid imagination." she said one day whilst she was shading in her eyebrows, peering in to the shaving mirror Dad had found on his tip.

"But it's like a mosaic," I tried to explain to her, "like thousands of bits of yours and other people's reflections in there, goodness only knows who you will see staring back at you."

"Oh that's awful! I don't know why you think them things," Mam said looking at me curiously.

I don't know either, I thought to myself then, as the memory faded, taking a last glance before I closed the bedroom door, blocking off that strange smell.

Within days Mike and I had settled in to our new flat and my health improved dramatically, as I wasn't catching coughs and colds all the time and we enjoyed the feeling of being in that comfortable space which reflected our style. Our friends and family visited us often and we reveled in feelings of cozy togetherness. It felt a long way from the disturbed house I'd grown up in, which I willed myself mentally to block out if I could; for the most part I'd stopped re-living the past, with the help of my Psychologist, who encouraged me to continue to write and journal my thoughts and feelings, especially the events of that last day when I had gone home seeking refuge, only to be told that there was 'no room at the inn'. The hurt of that still bore deep, like a discarnate entity sleeping in my guts.

On nights when Mike was working in his band, I was increasingly aware of my vulnerability as the pregnancy advanced and my due date was looming closer. The nearest telephone was half a block away and despite the couple downstairs reassuring us that they were on hand if we needed them, I was never convinced, especially when they were out a lot and when they weren't, they were busy doing other things loudly, which I was certain would keep them from answering the door.

I used to sit up waiting for Mike, sometimes long in to the early hours of the morning, which may have attributed to my insomnia which bothered me for years. Listening for the sound of the band's van, I would feel the faint movement from inside my tummy as our baby grew more and more still in advance of its birth. The hushed sound of stillness and my own heart beating was at times enough to strike fear in me, at the thought of what lay ahead and giving birth.

Every house has creaks and groans, when fires are turned off and the surround expands on the TV as it clicks, as if being switched back on and noisy water pipes rattle suddenly, but the sounds of this flat were unnerving, domineering even, I would say, in their timing, as if calculated to arouse my attention. By now I was used to feeling subtle energy changes, shifts in focus and awareness of 'presences' and I was fairly comfortable with it most of the time. However, I never felt particularly comfortable in that flat on my own. It unsettled me to the point of me going to sleep on the sofa with the lamp on. I never slept in the bedroom by myself even when Mike was in the flat. I sensed the nearness of Spirit like the presence of a slight breeze on a still afternoon. I became even more aware after reading a book called 'Voices in my Ear' by 'Doris Stokes'. It was perhaps through her that I came to accept my own ability to connect on a daily basis with the Spirit world but little did I know it then however, that I was about to be tested.

It was November the fifth, 'Guy Fawkes Night'. I stood at the bedroom window which looked out on to the road below and on to some bungalows where beyond them was an expanse of land, shrouded by a cavern of darkness. That night though, the place far in to the distance was iridescently lit from above by fireworks. I turned out the light in the bedroom so I could see them exploding and popping in the skies. I had felt colicky pains for most of the day and I was hoping it was the onset of labour. Mike had gone to the supermarket to buy us some sparklers and I had laid out a nice tea with sandwiches and a cake, to celebrate bonfire night.

After about ten minutes of watching, I felt my back ache so much that I had to sit down on the bed. I felt so weary I wanted to lie back, but after a second I realized uncomfortably that I was all alone in the bedroom in the pitch black and that the light switch was all the way on the other side of the wall. Turning on my knees, I inched my way over the bed, peering for clarity in the great loom of darkness for the light switch on the wall. Just as I was about to reach out and switch on the light, with uncanny timing, the door unnaturally creaked open, creating a halo from the dim light of the hall.

My senses fired up and I immediately felt my heart drum in wild arrest. I could almost hear it in my ears with uncontrolled panic. I continued to inch towards the door, seeing headlights from a car outside stream a flare through the window which comforted me briefly as it lit up the wall, but just as the light gathered, I could sort of make out an outline of someone standing in the doorway. This was like an eternal moment and that image is still with me and though I couldn't really tell, I sensed it was a woman. There was an objective quality about her presence, which I knew was not in my imagination and it both terrified and alarmed me. The intensity of the feeling rooted me to the spot, I dared scarcely to breathe. I sort of 'felt' her intention; it's difficult to explain, as though I was held in her consciousness or perhaps she in mine. It was indistinguishable either way and I knew that whoever it was, they weren't about to leave in a hurry.

Deliberately, slowly, I sat back resting against the head board, which momentarily eased my pelvic discomfort, vaguely feeling a hollowness and absence of breath, only a visceral reaction and something not unlike nausea gripped me, as I became aware of the odd sweet sickly odor of musty foist again; not an easy smell to describe, but one I have never forgotten. At once I was aware of a second presence enter the space where I was sitting, somewhat relieved it was one which I recognized, I was bathed in its familiarity, as it appeared to ease the darkness back and away from me, allowing me to suspend my fear and invite the Spirit to draw closer to me, if I had the courage. I watched the luminous strands of Akashic light, like tentacles seeking me out in the darkness and there I could see her more clearly, the bones on her skull shone like alabaster and the wisps of her coarse white hairs stood out as if brushing against my cheek, her breath which was cold lingered in the air like frost.

I dared myself to look in to her eyes. I prayed I would see tenderness there but the outline of her face and shoulders distracted me. She looked unusually tall, masculine even, without flesh, just bone as she appeared to waver in front of me, clothed in an indescribable drab garment, I could smell stale urine and hear a faint sound of her breathing croakily. When she saw me looking at her intently, she moved even closer, as though she was about to press her face in to mine. I was so scared, I didn't move. I wanted to get up but something told me to sit very still. She stood for just about a second, took one last look and then withdrew in to the shadows, leaving only the smell and a faint emotion of terrible sadness behind her.

*'The dark side of man's nature, allows him to remain earthbound by his senses'.*

I quickly grabbed an enveloped from on the top of the bedside table and frantically scribbled;

*'He sees only the physical material world around him and is blind to the reality. In his lucid moments of awareness, he is caught up in the breath of life, as it elevates him upon the flow of the winds and carries him timelessly upon the breeze, but on his descent in to the material world, he forgets the freedom such a thrill has given him and returns his thoughts once more to the basest of mortal attractions.*

*In his dreams, he is stirred by memories of flying high on the wings of immortality, he is shown great dances of light, swirling in iridescent hues, returning once more to the shores of the seas and his own silent emotion, awakening him to his nature and the language of his own heart, if only for a brief moment'*

I knew instinctively that this Spirit, whilst alive, had resided in our flat at some point, where for a long time she had haunted the space, perhaps, without even any memory of how she had come to be there. Her echo was so faint, as to be almost unperceivable by anyone, except for those with sensitivity of the Spirit world of which I was surely awakening to on a more regular basis. I sat suspended in a quality of reverence for what I had just seen and I felt reassured by the loving presence which had once again saved me from being annihilated by my own fears.

The experience of that moment developed further the strength within me that I would need for the journey which lay ahead and my communication with Spirit. It was then I realized and accepted the existence of the spiritual presence, which was always close at hand and entirely independent of me physically, whom I knew would remain steadfast in my life as a protection in times of great need.

Mike's banging of the door shut made me jump a little. I wondered if what had just taken place might bring on my labour, as the dull ache in my back increased, forcing me to take notice of it again. I didn't know how I was going to explain what I had just seen to Mike, not that I thought he would have trouble accepting it. Far from it, in fact, as Mike was opening up to the possibility of Spirit at quite a pace ever since his introduction in to the works of 'Edgar Cayce' 'The Sleeping Prophet'. We would often sit up at night and talk about it and even meditated together on occasion. We certainly prayed for good things for those we loved. Even so, I conceded, I wasn't sure he was quite ready for the idea of a ghost in our flat.

"I don't want you to do the gig tonight Mike, I don't feel so good." I blurted out to him when he turned on the light and popped his head round the door, his lovely face was a glow from the cold night air but I could see by his look, all apologetic, that he didn't have much choice.

"It's someone's birthday party, it's only a few hours, and we can't cancel at this late stage."

He stepped towards me to hug me, but even the gentlest of being held, hurt too much.

"I'm sick and tired of being on my own." I could feel the annoyance rise inside me and I twisted away from his embrace.

"Mam will come and stay," he tried to soothe. "It's only for a couple of hours," he said, "and I should be home for about..."

"Midnight!" I shouted as I swiped the envelope I'd been writing on, off the table childishly.

"I don't sodden care!" I said angrily, marching in to the bathroom, locking the door behind me.

I could hear Mike muttering to himself, exasperated. I sat tirelessly for what seemed a long while, exhausted at the finish from perching on the side of the bath, crying and blowing my nose in to a tissue.

"Come out darlin'," Mike was knocking on the door, "this is not good for you."

I slid the lock on the door, agreeing with him that he was right. I knew my anger wasn't good for anyone and increasingly of late, it seemed I was almost always upset over something. I accused Mike of being unfaithful to me; that theme of emotional abuse within the mind which ran like a stuck record in times of my insecurity. I told him that I suspected he was mucking about with other girls where he gigged, especially the 'Strippers' in the clubs on Sundays, 'filthy whores' I called them, though I knew full well he was committed to me, everyone said so, and I knew how he couldn't wait for the birth of our baby. Sadly, the reasoning and knowing on a logical level, never completely overrode the silent suppositions and emotional depression. Of course we made up as usual and our rifts rarely lasted more than an hour. He left for his gig that night in a more elevated mood.

The last bangs from fireworks faded in the distance and I turned off the television. It was especially cold that night so I turned the gas fire on to full blast and lay down on the sofa, drawing the quilt up to my chin. In seconds I was unable to keep my eyes open and I quickly fell in to a deep sleep.

It couldn't have been very long when I awoke to a feeling of complete body paralysis, something which has happened to me many times since then. This was my first experience of this sensation, which is extremely terrifying, where the mind wakes before the body has time to respond. Experts on the subject indicate that it's the body not moving smoothly through the stages of sleep with sustained sleep deprivation being one of the reasons for this common experience. I could testify to that, after lengthy periods of lack of sleep, when it appeared to happen more often.

For anyone who has ever experienced it for themselves, they will tell you that along with the paralysis there are often frightening sensations that can accompany it, such as sensing someone else in the room with you and even having the experience of something or someone pressing down on you usually with intent to harm. When I was aroused from sleep it was as if I was spinning in a vat of highly pressurized liquid, my head felt as if it was turning endlessly in a motion of ceaseless giddiness and I lay rooted to the spot, as if I was weighted down by an invisible force. I couldn't open my eyes or even move a single muscle. Internally I felt my entire muscles forcing themselves to move but it was absolutely useless.

Due to the regularity of the experience, over the years, I have done my own investigation in to the subject of sleep paralysis and though I have come to accept objectively, the theoretical explanations I have read by the experts, nevertheless, it remains somewhat an undisclosed mystery as far as I'm concerned, as to the physical phenomena that is often experienced by some whilst in that state.

That particular night, accompanying the paralysis, I heard a bang from above, as if from the light bulb, which jolted my senses awake. I sat up disorientated and almost immediately, I noticed the flames from the gas fire seemed oddly high and very yellow. The room temperature was very hot and I felt slightly sick with a mild headache.

Over the days that followed, Mike and I noticed we were getting headaches quite frequently whenever the fire was on full, but we didn't equate the physical problems we were experiencing with any particular source at that point, even though strange things began to happen when we were in the lounge watching TV with the gas fire on. For example a newspaper fell off the table on to the floor, lights flickered and the volume on the TV would suddenly increase; and once a loud clapping noise could be heard from behind and above us. One of the strangest things happened to Mike's Mum when she came to stay. She had been watching TV and dozed off. After about twenty minutes, she said she felt as if someone had taken hold of her shoulders from behind and pushed her forcefully off the sofa and when she woke up she was actually lying on the floor. She said her eyes were stinging slightly and she felt light headed and a little sickly. Whatever it was that was creating those unusual experiences seemed desperate to alert us to something that wasn't quite right.

Luckily for us it did, because a day later, a general inspection of the gas fire appliance revealed that the fire had been pouring out deadly Carbon Monoxide fumes and the gas fitter confided in us incredulously, saying that it was a miracle someone hadn't died in their sleep. He condemned it with red and black tape telling us he would inform our landlord immediately. I shuddered at the close call we'd all had with death.

The day after condemnation of our gas fire, my waters broke, in the middle of watching the sitcom 'Married with Children'. Mike's Mam and I had been chatting all evening. I laughed at something on the programme and then I felt a pop, and a pool of water trickled to my feet as I let out a nervous, excitable shriek and Mike's Mum who had been dozing, shot bolt upright.

"I think it's happening, my waters have broken!" I said as a tightness like a thick elastic band gripped me round the middle. Glancing at the clock I knew Mike's band would be well in to the second half by now, I wondered frantically how on earth I was going to let him know what was happening, as I wasn't even sure which club he was gigging at. Mike's Mum, as if reading my mind held out a piece of paper with the phone number of some place in Newcastle written on it.

"Mike left this before he went out," she said hurriedly. "I'll quickly pop downstairs and see if I can use Mark and Julie's phone."

I handed her the card with the hospital's number on it.

"Let the hospital know I think I'm in labour," I said, as another fairly tight band gripped my stomach.

I felt a sudden gear-change in myself, as if my entire body was thrust in to preparation for the inevitable slog that was ahead, though nervous I also felt abundant and alive as I cradled my belly, which felt smaller now the fluids had all but drained out.

The sound of Mike's Mum talking to the couple downstairs settled my nerves. I was so relieved that she was able to get them to answer the door, as most nights they were copulating by ten.

I stood in the lamp light of our room, just standing and looking, where the echoes of the past were there in the objects, the familiarity of things which drew to me comfort and security. I gently rocked the beautiful wooden crib all made up with cream, furnished with a little white furry rabbit which Mike had brought home the day before, smiling broadly as he placed it inside, pride pasted across his face. At that second, thoughts of my Grandmother Leah came to me, the softness of her face appeared in some interior within me, as though participatory in the miracle of guiding our baby's new life here.

'From generation to generation, all life begins with love'.

The words came to me and suddenly, I couldn't wait to meet our child, at that moment an exquisite and peaceful calm settled in me. I was ready.

Mike arrived at the hospital at midnight in a flurry of nervous excitement and November chill as I found out when he cuddled me, placing his freezing hands on my back where the hospital gown had become unloose, with a sharp intake of breath bringing on another painful contraction. I grappled for the gas and air, as wave upon wave of agonizing pain tore at my abdomen relentlessly.

Perhaps nature intelligently ordained for Birth to be violently painful, I considered, after it was all over. So that the transitory period of adjustment for both mother and child afterwards, is for the greater part mostly peaceful, as both settle in to their new lives together, acquainted by the harrowing experience they had both endured through the Birthing process; which is immeasurably life changing. Unconditional love must surely follow such an experience, I reflected, as I marveled at the beauty of this tiny little being who had come to the earth through us.

In the dim light of the hospital room, Mike and I gazed upon our beautiful daughter, Annelleise who I named after Anne Frank or Anneliese Marie Frank.

Annelleise Kathryn, our baby, peered up at us from the blanket she was swaddled in, her tiny hand gripped her Daddy's finger, alert, eyes wide. Even moments after being born, she had a look of intent, something that has always remained with her, that headstrong determination of hers revealed itself only minutes after entering the world and at that moment I knew her Spirit and I loved her like no other.

My stay in hospital was lengthened because of an Episiotomy, resulting in an infection, making the healing process long and difficult, but on my 21st Birthday, I was allowed to go home, cradling my Birthday gift from the Divine.

It was freezing cold, blankets of frost had turned everything white, visibility was poor and the taxi driver took almost an hour to get us home, by which time I was in agony from sitting but when we got there, it was well worth it. The lounge was full of balloons and Birthday and Congratulations cards which were lined side by side. Marie was there busily tidying round and making cups of tea for a few friends who had turned up to see me and the baby. There was one set back however, and quite a major one, which Mike had omitted to tell me.

Unfortunately the Landlord hadn't got round to fitting the new gas fire in the lounge, therefore due to the really cold spell, with temperatures down to minus degrees, we would have to live in our bedroom, for anywhere up to a month. Given in one hand and taken out of the other, I sighed. It felt surreal as we all piled in to our cramped bedroom, where the only source of heat was from mugs of tea in hand and the small two bar electric fire and lots of ahhs and ooohhhs from clucky visitors beaming at our sweet little bundle.

It was difficult doing everything in one cramped space, as we were having to dry clothes over a clothes horse in front of the fire, next to the baby's crib, which made the air damp and Annelleise was forever catching snuffles and colds. Looking back, I am sure it was the circumstances of the moisture and heat in that room at the beginning of her life that contributed to her Asthma when she was two. The landlord's wife explained after numerous attempts to contact him, that her husband had gone on a long holiday to India, reassuring us that his priority was to install our new gas fire upon his return. In all honesty, I didn't know whether I could wait that long.

It was a bitterly cold November, a month which seemed to go on endlessly. We only ventured in to the back kitchen to make meals and bring them back in to the bedroom. I never went out without Annelleise, not even to the front gate of our yard to put the rubbish out but as Christmas approached, and the ice was too thick on the pavements for the pushchair, I decided I would venture to the shops to buy a little gift for Mike. I got to the end of the lane and panicked. What if she needed feeding? My mind reeled with thoughts. What if she woke up and felt afraid because I wasn't there? I was attaching my own fears that I had had as a child on to my daughter. It made me feel wretched but after minutes I reassured myself that Mike was perfectly capable of looking after his own daughter and anyway, I had to strive for her to become independent and not rely upon me for happiness. So I pushed the irksome worries to one side and carried on to the shops.

The feeling and nearness of Spirit seemed to grow stronger, perhaps it was because of my entering a period of maturity or perhaps because I needed their strength more than ever. I'm not sure but the presence of the 'living energy' helped me to cope with the difficult situation. For ten weeks we had to more or less live in the bedroom, which occasionally would fill up with that horrible smell of damp musk, when I sensed the nearness of 'her' the Spirit who had unnerved me on bonfire night and whom I felt silently watched on.

I neglected everyone at that time, as my only focus was on my child. Mike's needs were lost at the bottom of a pile of 'to do' lists I mentally wrote every morning I awoke. I couldn't even remember the last time we'd kissed. Sometimes I was so wrapped up in the wellbeing on my child that I felt I was going out of my mind with worry about her. I searched through books and collected leaflets at the Health Clinic on babies and nutrition and immunizations and anything else I could get my hands on.

"She's perfectly normal!" my Health Visitor screeched in her high-pitched, Wearside accent, when I attempted to explain my concerns to her at the Health Clinic that day.

Maureen she was called, with a particularly whiney voice that tailed off at the end of a sentence. Clearly she was exasperated by my visits to her office as it was the fourth that week. As I talked, she scribbled frantically and then looked at me the way a dog does at its owner when it cocks its head from side to side in a sort of pleading way. Perhaps she was hypnotizing me, I smiled to myself, as I closed her room door behind me, satisfied once again that my little girl was healthy and I was just neurotic.

The cold bore deep as I mincingly made my way on the ice up the steep bank to our flat. I sincerely hoped it would be our only Christmas in there and it was made worse by our new neighbour who had moved in to Julie and Mark's flat downstairs. He stared at me vacantly from between the vertical blinds with an expression I couldn't read and when I waved cheerily his way, he didn't bat an eyelid. He gave me the creeps.

I saw the warm glow from the Christmas tree lights in the bedroom window upstairs and it looked lovely I thought and despite the hardship of living in one room, we had managed to create an inviting little place. When I got in Mike was sellotaping down the corners of a present.

"Didn't hear you come up," he said, as I bent down and kissed the top of his head.

He was wrapping up Annelleise's dolly and eating a stick of peppermint candy. He smelt of Christmas.

"They've cancelled that gig for tonight," he carried on, folding the paper neatly. "Another weather warning apparently," he said. I gleefully kissed him again.

I tossed my coat on to the bed and lifted Annelleise up from the changing mat on the floor. She smiled lively.

"I think I'll make us some lovely bread and butter pudding," I said glancing over at Mike. "I think we should eat it in bed watching telly and when baby sleeps," I teased, knowing Mike was watching me. "Then you and I should have some yumminess of our own," I said a little provocatively.

It had been ages since we did anything together and recently I had noticed that Mike was looking a bit down. It had escaped me how underweight he was, I thought, seeing how big his jumper looked on him.

The next morning a man from the County Council knocked and when I opened the door he handed me some official looking papers, while smiling broadly from a fleshy, cold, red face. I was in my dressing gown and my hair was a mess after the night

Mike and I had spent in bed together. It was also freezing again, I complained, as a cloud of cold air escaped from outside in to the hall way. Hurriedly I grabbed the papers from the man, cheerily shouting "Thanks!" as I closed the door behind him and ran quickly back upstairs in to our warm bedroom.

I couldn't take in what he had he just told me. Were we being offered a two bedroom house on that nice Council estate up by the old Vicarage? I wondered excitedly as I stopped inside the doorway of our bedroom to read the letter. Yes, we were! I threw the letters up in the air and twirled round falling softly next to Mike and Annelleise who were snuggled in together deep in the duvet.

"We've got a house!" I sang in to his ear. His eyes opened wide and he beamed like a satellite. This was just what we'd both been praying for.

Later that night, behind closed eyes, I could see light from the moon, as it shone through the bedroom window. I had spent most of the day cleaning and packing our things into boxes and had been exhausted when I had fallen asleep around nine p.m. Faint muffled sounds from Annelleise in her crib alerted me. Mike must've fallen asleep on the settee, I thought trying to feel if the bed was empty beside me. I was so tired, I could barely move. What time was it even, I wondered as I struggled to wake up. I had been restless during the night worrying about how we would be able to afford the move to our new house.

Annelleise again made a muffled sound from her crib, which I hadn't heard her make before, it sounded as if she was trying to cry. I turned on my side to get up but my body felt unusually weighty as if it was being held down. I struggled to move but I couldn't, it was as if every ounce of strength had left me. Sleep paralyses had struck me again, I thought frantically. In the stillness I could hear my child struggling to breathe, gasping, I could hear her. Oh my God! I thought desperately. Mike! I tried to shout but words wouldn't come out, I couldn't even move my eyes. I was rooted to the spot, unable to move a muscle.

It seemed like minutes passed, but it must have only been a few seconds when something extraordinary happened, I shall never forget. Behind my closed eyelids appeared the old woman, the 'Spirit' I had first seen on Bonfire Night. The alabaster of her skin was bathed in warm light, her features were soft and faint, like a pencil outline, and she wavered like paper in a breeze. She leaned over me, I could see the hollowness of her eyes as she got closer and closer until she was so close I could feel her breath on my face and then suddenly, with force, she took hold of my shoulders and pulled me up so hard, I could feel her fingers and bones in my flesh. I felt myself being thrust forwards and I was thrown on to the floor. I was shaking.

I quickly lifted Annelleise up, she was breathing fast, she felt hot, beads of sweat were covering her face, she was distressed, somehow she had managed to pull the blankets over her head, but being on her tummy, she couldn't move her head away from the blankets to get air. I quickly removed her clothing and bathed her in tepid water until she was cool again and I rocked her gently for what seemed an age, until she fell back to sleep. I couldn't believe what I had just experienced. In the stillness of the room, I still sensed the Spirit's energy although I could no longer see her. Warm tears fell and I silently thanked her. How could I not feel such enormous gratitude? She had helped me and my child. I don't know what would've happened if I hadn't been able to wake up. Would Annelleise have been unable to breathe? I didn't dare contemplate. In those day's people still lay babies down on their tummies to sleep, unaware at that time, of the danger of Cot Death.

I will eternally be grateful to the Spirit/Soul who helped me that day. Wherever she is, I wish her peace.

In the weeks that followed, we were given the keys to our new home. Mike decorated it beautifully with money from his Grandparents who had been extremely supportive to us the entire time. Mike had amazed me with his DIY talents, wall-papering, tiling, laying carpets, and all done to a high standard. Mike's choice in furnishings were tasteful, mine, rather more bohemian, however, it was an exciting eclectic mix of flare and urban modesty. We moved in fully when the crocuses were in full bloom, their glossy purple petals adorned our front and back gardens and dark green privet hedging grew thick between our house and the next door neighbours. I glanced at the garden as the wind whipped the sheets on the washing line and I smiled, I was very content. Sometimes those inner feeling set you alight with strange and wonderful thoughts of the future. Somehow I always knew that that house was going to be a happy home, it felt so far removed from my former life that I could have easily forgotten it had ever existed.

I cleaned meticulously and each evening when Annelleise was in her cot, I took out my journals and jotted down thoughts that sprung to mind. There was an ease that I had never felt before, not only with my writings but in every area of life. I had friends and was beginning to feel a part of a wider community and I started to investigate other religions and seek out like minded souls. The Spiritualist Church had become a place where I would occasionally go and meet people, however in truth, I never saw or heard anything that made me believe the Mediums I saw there were really connecting with the higher Spiritual planes or that the information they were receiving was from reliable sources. I was seeking to understand, but perhaps looking in all the wrong places.

I used to come away from the services feeling that there was something inherently missing. I questioned the validity of the messages that were being given, at times so trivial, I wondered why Spirit would go to such lengths to 'tell Aunty Milly, her earring has fallen down the loo' or that 'Joe ought to change his three piece suite, because Ada (his wife in Spirit) complained it was looking a bit shabby'. Nevertheless, it allowed me to develop my awareness in an environment I thought was embracing of this phenomena.

Unfortunately, however, I was to learn the hard way that the Church wasn't the way my spirit wanted to take me. I was meant to sit alone to receive the writings. After all I'd been doing it all my life, and it wasn't until I experienced some rather frightening psychic phenomena that I learnt the first golden rule of Spiritual Law, which came to me while relaxing. 'Never force that which is latent within, to develop. Like a seed in the soil, it cannot be hurried to grow'.

I questioned the founder of the Spiritualist Church one day, without realizing it, by doing so, I had tiptoed into quarters that were very much areas of no entry. We had sat for 'development' in the back room, about five of us in a circle around a small table in the dark, with only a candle in the corner giving minimal illumination. Closing our eyes, we were asked to hold hands, relax and go within. I wasn't entirely sure what I was meant to do, so I absorbed the stillness, setting aside any reticence I was feeling and sort of drifted into that comfortable place of tranquility that I was used to. Within moments, the sound of the table's legs knocking against the floor, made me jump.

"Let what is meant to happen, happen," said the Founder in a voice which no longer resembled his own. His accent had changed, it sounded Asian, it startled me and my eyes quickly opened.

In hindsight, I wished I had kept them shut tight, as I saw in the glow of the candlelight, the table which had been in the center, was now slowly swaying side to side, suspended, a few inches off the floor. I glanced around at everyone else, though difficult to see, they all seemed oblivious to the table which was becoming more and more erratic in its swaying.

"Does anyone here have a message for any of us!?' the Founder asked, his voice booming, making me jump again.

The table which had appeared to dance all by itself, settled back on to the floor quite effortlessly.

Mrs. Clark, who had been holding my hand, suddenly flounced forward in her chair, lifeless. A mere wisp of a woman in her sixties, who played the organ every Monday and ran the tuck shop for the Church, she, after a few seconds, adopted a larger than life personality.

"Good evening friends!" she said affectively, characteristic of a compere in a theatre play house. No longer was she the shy, retiring, demure lady serving teas; here she was bold and extrovert, waving her hands to elaborate on each word spoken.

"I'm very happy to be here," she said, addressing us all. I glanced around, noticing that all eyes were still closed. "It's taken me a long time to get here," she announced with a certain melancholy. I wondered what she meant by that. Was she referring to her own life getting here, as Mona Clark? I wondered. Or that of the Spirit of Lucile Jeffrey's who she told us she was that evening. Who at aged thirty three had suffered from an infectious disease which had begun in her leg and had spread to her lungs, where in 1878 she had died at her beloved Shaftesbury Theatre in Covent Garden, where she had sang opportunistically since she had been a small child.

I listened intently, mesmerized by Mrs. Clark's sweeping gestures and gregarious laughter, as she recounted moments of her mostly pleasurable life on earth. I could have listened for much longer but after indulging in her discourse for around ten minutes or so, the Founder of the Church, who appeared to have lost his Asian accent and in broad Geordie, told us all to "Come back and be fully present in the room." Lucile Jeffrey's zapped back in to Mrs. Clark or to wherever she had come from and Mrs. Clark once again assumed her small mouse-like demeanor.

When we sat around the tea table later, I made a point of sitting next to the Founder so I could ask him about the extraordinary levitating table which was far weirder, I thought, than Mrs. Clark's glamorous alter ego who I respectively acknowledged was plausible. 'Weird' was the word I had used that apparently the Founder later told me was 'inapprehensible' and because of it, he told me "I was little more than a novice and clearly not ready to become a Medium."

I was absolutely flabbergasted. I had enquired about the nature of the phenomena I had witnessed, deliberately trying not to express my suspiciousness and in fact I had calculatedly worded my question so that I didn't come across as offensive or rude. After half an hour of feeling uncomfortable, listening to everyone twitter on about what they were having for tea, to so and son's funeral, everything but the events that had just taken place, I couldn't hold my tongue a second longer. I announced to the group that I would not be returning and told them I believed they were missing an opportunity to discuss the meaning and validity of the phenomena that had just taken place, and surely that was the point of the development meetings. Disapproving looks I ignored, as I purposefully took my time to zip up my coat and put on my hat and slipped out the front door, uttering "Bye" under my breath.

Over the next few weeks I began to wonder how much of the condition of Schizophrenia was linked to the blockages in energy flows within the meridians of the body, through use of toxic substances or negative fields of thought transferences or psychic manipulation of supernatural energies and forces, which I believed were being impressed upon me at the Church at that last meeting. It came out of the blue one morning as I remember, just as I awoke, I heard voices, like a stream of chattering from out of a radio, only they weren't on the radio, they were inside my head. This happened several times over a course of a week and then I began having severe vertigo.

One day I had to ring my Sister Marie to come and look after Annelleise for me as I couldn't even stand up, which lasted for almost two days. I was experiencing strange feelings throughout my body, sometimes tingles like goose flesh, then cool draughts from out of nowhere would blow through my hair. The worst was the sleep paralysis. It happened with timed regularity every night I fell asleep and almost always it was accompanied by horrible sensations of something holding me down, grotesque shapes and images which took me back to when I was a child and the night terrors I experienced.

Even more startling were the marks on my arm one day I woke up. I was beginning to think that I was having some kind of psychotic episodes. I didn't dare show Mike for fear he would think me insane. I was already wondering that myself. I decided to stop spiritual activities altogether. I stopped associating with people from the Spiritualist Church and I stopped reading Literature about World Religions and Theology and the New Age Movement and even to a degree stopped writing in my journal. Instead I focused on things that were lighter hearted, like Theatre. I joined the local Amateur Dramatic Society and threw myself wholeheartedly into performing in plays, farce, comedies, anything, in which to take my mind off strange psychic experiences.

To be truthful, I was deeply afraid and didn't like the unusual occurrences that had happened to me. I didn't understand it. I longed to talk to Mam about it, just to get her no-nonsense opinion on it all and even though I knew she wouldn't comprehend it, I so wanted to see her. I missed her so much; it felt like I hadn't been home in ages.

Several nights later, I sat at the bedroom window overlooking the hump of land that separated me from Mam. I could see the tiny silvery lights that marked the road up past the old Railway Station, winding their way to where Mam and Dad's house was. In my mind's eye, I could visualize them sleeping. I could picture the garden, a glow in street light, with Dad's piles of scrap stacked up in sacks by the front door and Rebel, their Alsatian, tethered on a long chain asleep in the shed. As though I was there, hovering above the roof, I could see the fields stretching for miles.

I had distanced myself from them and home. Even the word was difficult to say. Regret surfaced in me, shoving itself to the forefront of my mind, evoking such strong emotions. Was I always going to feel so torn? I wondered, afflicted by guilt? Even when my life had turned a corner, revealing wonderful opportunities, I still remained fearful of the hold that that house and Dad had over me. I viewed the objects in our bedroom, the neat, and orderliness of things and pictured in my mind the contrast and disarray of Mam's surroundings and it made me so sad. I hoped she was alright but I had to protect myself from hurt, I couldn't go back just yet.

I glanced at the clock, it was almost four a.m. I reached beneath the bed and pulled out the jotter containing snippets of thoughts and sojourns into distant realities. It was like a comforting friend, like all my diaries had been. I held it in my hands, took hold of the pen and allowed thoughts to impress themselves upon my mind. In a sort of twilight repose, with ease, I wrote speedily.

*'What deters life from progressing? Is it the inability to make a decision that corresponds with issues of a material nature, because of attachment and fear for our physical wellbeing? Is it a binding we have forced upon ourselves to restrict us from making a decision which may alter the course of our life? And what if we do nothing? Will life still progress, as though a natural law exists, shaping the life, regardless of our efforts?*

*If we believe, that within us there is a governance, a part of our being, thus being the 'Soul' which has an over-view perspective, can we therefore accept that this spiritual faculty of 'Seeing' is capable of bringing about the necessary changes, we must make, in order to bring about and restore peace?*

*If we choose to disbelieve that fundamentally we are 'Spirit' in origin, then this particular argument has little or no validation and we are at the mercy of our rational ego and therefore all that presents itself in life, are mere obstacles to climb over.*

*If on the other hand, we accept that a 'Spiritual Self' is in existence within us, then we must also consider that this 'Spiritual Self' is the governing aspect, which has attracted the circumstances of our reality in order to learn and become more whole in all aspects. To be at the mercy of the ego, implies that we are more or less only capable of physical functioning. Yet if we consider that we are much more than just our physical beings and that we can operate or at least are capable of operating, on finer levels of awareness outside the realm of our five senses, which serve the purpose for our existence in a physical world. May we therefore accept that there are extra sensory organs, though not present by the physical eye, nonetheless exist within us and allow us to 'See',*

*'Hear' and 'Sense 'all existing realms outside the physical realm and that our 'Emotional body' is capable of experiencing these other 'Transcendental States of BE~eing? That our 'Spirit Body' is always aware of the finer densities of vibrational matter of these other or outer Realities?'*

I rested my pen, breathing in the subtle energies of twilight in our room. How long I'd been writing, I had no idea. It felt like moments, but the clock showed half an hour had passed. I had no notion where this writing was taking me; it was as if a magic wand had been waved in front of my mind and erased any memory of me having written it. Extraordinary, I knew, was the way in which it expressed itself, benign and reassuring, like a quiet voice of kindness in response to my tempestuous and troubled thoughts.

The newness of that spring brought with it the changes and colours and bright sparks of life amongst the leafy litter. Hyacinths, daffodils and blue bells, English flowers so delicately beautiful they could take your breath away, edged the grass verges and gardens. Bird song filtered out the hum of distant traffic and Annelleise's yellow bonnet shone in the sunlight as she sat upright in her pushchair, as I wheeled her over stones on the mucky path around the back of St Thomas's Church ground; past the tall oak, the long way back from the shops. It did us both good, our cheeks were rosy and Annelleise was a contented baby for it. The half an hour or so from getting off the beaten track gave me time to take in nature and to stop at different places along the route and show Annelleise the beauty of life. My daughter would also appreciate the splendors of the world, from the moment of her birth, I pledged to pass on to her the rich lineage of our families forbearers and the faith and love she had been born in to.

That day, however, we wouldn't be going straight home after the shops. We were taking the bus up to Gran and Granddad's, now that I had laid to rest the previous upsets. I wanted my child to have her Grandparents, even if my Dad was the most unlikely Grandfather anyone ever could have, him still wielding heavy scrap metal over his shoulders, sporting tattoos and cursing the Establishment. According to my sisters, he was as unpredictable as ever and they chose only to visit when he was out at the tip. I was looking forward to seeing Marie, Clare and Ann. I missed our closeness. Marie's daughter was as sweet as sugar, Clare also had a little girl who was very petite and Ann now had a robust son.

The bus dropped us off at the corner of our road, near my old Infant's School. Annelleise was snuggled in her blanket fast asleep. It was as if nothing had really changed, I thought, seeing some of our old neighbours, still as nosey. I smiled, seeing their nets twitch when I pushed open our garden gate.

I opened the kitchen door excitedly and Clare spotted me first and excitedly twirled me round while whispering in my ear "Look through the window in the garden." She squeezed my shoulders pushing me in that direction. An enormous Rottweiler was salivating over a Pig's knuckle, growling and tossing it in the air. When it saw me there, it ran and jumped at the window barking so loud, it woke up the babies.

"Oh my God," I said, quickly pulling the curtains closed. "Where's Rebel?"

I hardly needed to ask. I shouldn't have been as surprised as Dad had been talking about getting rid of Rebel because his legs were bad.

"It's Mam and Dad's new dog," Clare whispered, with a look of real concern.

"Why on earth can't he get a dog that's not vicious?" I protested at Mam incredulously. "What about the children?" I went on, feeling my insides scream in frustration.

"It doesn't bite apparently," Mam said, seeing the look on all our faces.

"It's ridiculous!" Ann moaned loudly.

"Is it gonna be allowed in to the house, Mam?" I pleaded, knowing full well that the answer was going to be yes.

Mam loved animals, she was a natural giver and anyway, even if she had protested, it wouldn't have done any good.

"Your Dad wants it to," she nodded, answering me.

I looked at the thick hairs and muddy paw marks all over the carpet and instantly knew that I would never let Annelleise crawl around in all that muck. The dog's bark was so deep and loud and terrifying, it was as if it was trying to burst through the back door.

"Can't you ask Dad to send it back, Mam?" I asked, seeing her look of silent acceptance of the situation.

I knew it was futile and even though there were five Grandchildren to consider, as Thomas also had a Son, I knew that Mam had little choice in the matter in reality. Dad had decided and that was that. My sisters and I just looked at one another. Nothing more needed to be said, as we knew that a decision had already been made; the dog had been chosen over us. He had known that it had been given to an Animal Sanctuary by its owners because it had tried to bite one of their children, we found out later. Unfortunately, because of Dad's need to have the doors wide open whenever he was at home meant we wouldn't be able to visit when he was in and because of his flexible working hours, we would never know when he would arrive back, therefore the dog would freely roam in the house.

Sadly, that was to be the last day my sisters and I would all meet up again with our children at Mam and Dad's. It was the last time we'd all be together at home. Mam, sadly, would be denied the closeness of her Grandchildren because Dad would never let her out of his sight long enough for her to forge a close relationship with them.

I felt that we had once again taken a huge blow, much like a break in a bone, only it wasn't so easily mended. Our needs were not considered and the hopes we all had, to raise our children to value the family and family life, were sadly never to be realized. It would be at least twenty years or more before we would feel that semblance of a normal family life again, but not before the tissue, sinew and blood had been torn away from the bones of love.

# Chapter Six

## *Spirit*

"Hang on to hope." The voice gently prevailed within my mind but I dismissed it, willing the threshold of atonement to be crossed and for my Dad to fall even further in to the susceptibility of darkness. Perhaps there, I thought to myself, he would actually meet the devil himself, I scoffed, as the mood of resentment, then self-recrimination gathered. I felt bereft. Perhaps given enough disappointment, it is entirely possible to come to expect it, like a Grim Reaper, making an appearance silently, unannounced, but with ominous presence of looming fates. I wanted to turn back and appeal to Mam, to tell her that she had to put her foot down and start living her own life but something inside stopped me. I knew Dad's wishes were imposed upon her and it was survival that made her silently relent, to recede into the background of life, blanched in to insignificance from years of being molded in to passivity, downtrodden by a force much greater than she was able to withstand.

I chose to walk home and thankfully Annelleise was completely oblivious to my sadness, as she clapped and sang jumbled words of a nursery rhyme. She was generous with smiles to strangers and people couldn't help being enthralled by her. Her happy chatter brought me back to the present moment and I acknowledged how blessed I was and thanked unseen forces who had brought her to me. Yet anger and frustration registered more powerfully within and fixed tight a hold to my mood. By the time I got home I was ready to scream. I looked for Mike, so that he could take Annelleise to enable me to shut myself away and vent my anger, but I remembered he told me he was seeing an old friend that day and wouldn't get home until late.

Thankfully Annelleise contented herself easily so I was able to vent some frustration and beat the pillow, silently crying so that she didn't hear me. But from every pore of my being, it hurt. I didn't know how I could change any of it, perhaps that was the worst, and the injustice overwhelmed me. I didn't know how I could free Mam from his clutches and the responsibility of it was too much to cope with.

How can you make any plans, I cried to myself, when every road you walk down is blocked? I didn't know how to carry on and live with the internal pain and bondage. Who could I turn, to make things better? Was there anyone who understood what it was like to be this immobilized by pain and resentment? Could I take a pill to alleviate it?

In the moments that followed the releasing of such deep emotion, not so much consciously, but out of desperation and from the sanctum or part of me that would forever be untouched, I resounded to build a more solid wall around my emotions so that no one would ever hurt me again. The rest of me, the part who lived and breathed, I couldn't care less about anymore. 'She' my Spiritual Self, whoever 'She' was, who kept my life moving forward, could do as she pleased, for she would never hurt so deeply again, that I decreed. No one alive and breathing would ever steal her into those alleyways of deception and grotesque again, not without her consent, completely free she would exist from now on, on her terms.

Some months later, life seemed to turn a corner, as it does when the deeply buried hurts stop reigning their tyrannical power over you. I realized how fortunate I was. Mike was still doing gigs and he had also began working away from home with his Dad in their Roofing business and the vigor that we poured in to our home also spilled out in to many areas of our life, including our relationship with each other. Mike worked tirelessly but despite it, he looked well. Our conversations deepened as we were both curious about the Spirit and the existence of life after death. Mike still found revelations in the books of 'Edgar Cayce'.

The months passed steadily and our relationship at that time, I believed, was good, or so I thought. We meditated together and occasionally prayed and often spent time in the evenings just talking. At that time, my writings had tapered off, as though the expression was flowing down other channels, satisfying my inborn restlessness to journey within the recesses of mind.

However as time went by, it soon became evident when Mike came home after a long stretch away, how unhappy that he had really become. Something had changed. Sometimes I'd catch him sitting in a pensive mood just staring in to space, looking quite depressed. When I asked him what was wrong, he couldn't tell me, except to say that he found working with his Dad very difficult. I couldn't dispute how different they both were. Mike was a natural communicator whilst his Dad found even the most mundane of small talk, difficult.

Out of the blue, one day, Mike told me that he wasn't going back to work with his Dad again. He'd sat quietly upstairs for nearly two hours, thinking, and then when he finally came down, he said he couldn't do it anymore. A part of me felt disappointed as I had grown accustomed to having money, which was a reprieve from the years of nothingness.

When I pressed Mike to tell me why, he just broke down and cried.

There was an ocean of words unsaid in the silence that followed. I knew Mike was a creative and introspective person who had experienced a lot of anguish as a result of his Mother and Father's unconventional marriage, where his Dad spent months on end away from home for most of Mike's life. I remember the overwhelming sadness he experienced, when he found out his Father had been leading a 'double life' even having a son and partner in another part of the country. The devastation and impact it had on his family was catastrophic, it took a very long time for them to come to terms with it and even longer for their forgiveness. He couldn't communicate with his Dad about anything, so different they both were, but part of me hadn't really considered any of that.

When I had encouraged him to work away, all I could think about was the ease and comfort that we would all experience, financially. Perhaps a part of me had stopped caring, not taking in to account Mike's feelings and I felt disgusted in myself when I noticed a small sore on his ear which he said wasn't healing up, I knew was due to stress. I looked at Mike in the doorway, he had lost weight and I was ashamed to admit, that I hadn't really noticed it until then, his brown eyes weren't as vibrant as usual and he looked notably drawn.

"There's a job going at the Cable Factory," he said, halfheartedly, taking a cigarette from out of the box, lighting it. He opened the front door, blowing the smoke outside. "The Foreman said the job's mine if I want it," he said, before inhaling long on the cigarette. "Moneys not great but I could get a few more gigs with the band." He looked at me, waiting for my reaction.

I couldn't see Mike in a factory, he was different from the men in the village who drank in the Social Club and wore football shirts on match days.

"Well, if you think you could do it," I said, rubbing my hand on his shoulder. "But what does it entail?" I asked, hoping to sound enthusiastic.

"Making sure the cable is straight and goes on to the drum properly," he responded with a warranted sigh. "Not too taxing or anything," he said attempting to pull a face and make me laugh. "I could try it at least until something better comes a long," he continued, stubbing the cigarette out on the wall.

I saw the determination, his unyielding exterior, hiding his fears as he tried so hard to do for my sake. He cuddled me to him, but my mind was trammeled by doubt and uncertainty.

Annelleise by now had blossomed in to a beautiful child, with golden, cascading ringlets that danced with every sweep of her robust frame. She had a vivaciousness and curiosity of life which compelled others to her and her personality lit up the room whenever she was present. Sometimes when she woke up from her afternoon nap, I would hear her chattering as if to someone and when I glanced in to her room she would be standing, holding out her toy, clearly in animated discourse. One such afternoon, just as I was about to enter her room, I saw what I thought looked like a lady, dressed in a very beautiful long, pale, lemon, corseted dress of such grace and elegance. She was holding a parasol and the image of her was so faint and vanished so quickly, I wondered if I'd imagined it.

Annelleise turned to me and so matter of fact she said, "You're not my real Mummy… you're my Mummy… but you're not my real Mummy," and when she saw how surprised and sad I was, she cuddled me lovingly. Many nights I woke to hear her chattering to someone in her bedroom. Sometimes she told me that an old man with very white hair and white beard appeared to her and told her about a place called 'Dazzling land' where she said, in her innocence, that the old man tended to a garden, where there were flowers of every colour and that it was so beautiful, and with such innocence as only children can portray, she wistfully said to me, "Though he has a long thick coat that nearly touches the floor, he doesn't have any shoes Mummy."

Many years later, I met some wonderful people who introduced me to the Bahia Faith and showed me a photograph of 'Abdul Baha' the Son of 'Bahaullah', Founder of the Faith and upon looking at it, Annelleise began to cry as she told me that it was a picture of the man she had seen all those years ago as a child, whom took her in her dreams to the beautiful garden of iridescent flowers of every colour.

That summer rolled by, certain and positive like a child. I threw myself in to creative ambitions, making lovely our home and engaging Annelleise in lots of fun activities. I had never felt more certain of our futures, so much so, that I was considering stopping taking the contraceptive pill in the hope that I would fall pregnant with another baby. I'm not certain looking back, if Mike agreed whole heartedly to another baby at that time in our lives. We talked about it but Mike was so heavily burdened by responsibilities for the family and our futures that he could never give a definitive yes or no. I felt sure it was right and believed that Annelleise would benefit from a brother or sister. I felt in my heart that it was the right time.

Mike expressed his worries about money as it was always an issue between us. I spent it like I had an Aladdin's lamp but Mike was more cautious and sometimes our arguments became deeply personal and devastatingly destructive. I rolled over the arguments as a gymnast might, in training on the high beam, but Mike on the other hand struggled. I was unaffected by them, I had grown up hearing my parent's shattering and crushing of each other in their worded wars. Even my Psychologist admitted it was understandable that I considered it perfectly 'normal' but Mike recoiled after our lengthy shouting and seemed to almost enter a depressive state which could last for days on end.

I knew that questions about our mutual compatibility to stay together scoured deep in to his psyche. Don't ask me how I knew, I just did. I didn't fear the future whatever it held, not then or ever. A part of me embraced whatever the universe doled out. I couldn't imagine that it would ever be as self-sacrificial as the past. My hard and separated heart had anchored itself in distrust, perhaps it was because of this and my staggeringly simple attitude to the fates, that Spirit and Angels unexpectedly transmitted their cascade of heavenly reality upon me. I could never have prepared myself for it but luckily, I was receptive. For in actuality, it was me who had the threshold to cross.

Mike's job at the Cable factory ended, last to come he was first to go when economic strife hit. I was somewhat relieved, as it was a reprieve not to see him looking unhappy, as months of endless night shifts, watching cables wind on to a drum and feeling more and more isolated from his work mates, had taken its toll on his physical and mental health. Reluctantly he signed on to the dole, but it was a period of simultaneous setbacks, one too many that shunted him in to a place of condensed isolation. I had learnt to cope with many things, but seeing a man in such despair was one I had no experience of. I could apprehend anger, rage and retribution and I willed Mike to draw upon these forces to drag himself out of his depression but his way was different to mine.

I shifted uneasily in the Doctor's waiting room, as Annelleise played happily, absorbed by the coloured bricks she was stacking on top of one another. I kept noticing other couples as they walked in or ones sitting together quietly chatting, I felt like my heart was about to burst with sorrow. I knew I was pregnant, I didn't need a piece of paper to tell me, but the doctor's receptionist insisted I had to come to the surgery to receive my results. Somewhere within my Soul I had felt such enormous joy when I'd missed my period for a second month but from the hollow part, a place of shuttered rooms where unrealized dreams lay indistinguishable, I saw my shadow, the part of me which I had built the walls around whom I knew was unreachable, so far buried she was beneath mountains of hurt. I could've cried right there and then, realizing that the future which I'd clung on to with Mike was all but ebbing away and I didn't know how to stop it. I cried inside myself. I loved him so much but I didn't believe in myself enough to trust it.

Carrying the piece of paper in my pocket, I held Annelleise's hand tightly as we slowly walked the long way round past the shops, the way we both liked. Away from the beaten track, the cars slowly crept, because of black ice forming on the roads as dark descended. I was carrying a tiny spark of life within me and my spirit was overjoyed. I held the vision of the tiny beating of my baby's heart within my mind and I prayed to Spirit that they would help us to work it all out. I didn't know if I had the strength to go it alone, but if it was their will that I had to, I asked only that they would aid me to do so.

Mike was sprinkling salt on the path as I carried Annelleise over the doorstep. I would assess his mood before telling him the news, I thought as I unbuttoned Annelleise's coat. She was falling asleep so I lay her on the settee and followed Mike in to the kitchen. I thought that he seemed a little brighter. He had lit incense and some calm and chilled music was sounding from the CD player.

"I've taken a job with my Dad at Sellafield Power Station in Cumbria. I'm getting picked up at ten tonight so we can be on site first thing in the morning," he said, turning to me. I was stunned. "I'll be away a few weeks," he spoke, looking more certain than he'd done in ages. "I know I said I wasn't goin' to," he said slowly, "but, its money. I can't carry on like this, I feel like a piece of shit… I just want to do what's right Diane." He trailed off. "I mean…." He turned to me again, searchingly, "I don't even know if we're okay anymore," he said looking at me as if trying to read my thoughts. "It's all just going fuckin' wrong," he said loudly.

I shushed him and closed the kitchen door, so that Annelleise wouldn't hear us. I didn't want our daughter to grow up hearing arguments like I'd had to. At least until now, Mike and I had only fought when she was asleep. Mike carried on talking, ignoring my annoyance at him for raising his voice.

"You know…. I haven't a clue what I can do long term. Everywhere you hear people are being laid off and businesses shutting down, but I want to better myself for Annelleise and you," he said, taking a cigarette out of the box, opening the kitchen window. "I don't want us to live in a crap Council house," he said, his face giving way to his true feelings. "I hate that this is all I can provide, I feel like I've failed…"

I watched him, he seemed to be trembling slightly, I could feel tears coming but I suppressed them. I don't know if it was the smell of the food Mike was cooking or the intensity of emotion, but I rushed to the bathroom to vomit and each time I tried to leave, I wretched again. It seemed like ages before I felt well enough to go downstairs. I could hear Mike giving Annelleise her supper and getting her ready for bed. I could hear them chattering to each other, Mike singing and playing her a song on his guitar and her clapping with joy. It should've been a moment of happiness and yet I seemed unable to muster any feelings whatsoever. I could feel only the part of me that stepped in and out of that comfortable place, drift momentarily, where the stark colours were replaced by soft hues of mutable light, as I sought a few moments of stillness of mind and at some place of soul, I appealed to the 'Great Spirit' for help.

Later when Annelleise was asleep in her bed, I stretched out in the soft suds in the bath and thought of what Mike said before he had left. I repeated his words over and over in my mind. "I want it to work between us, but is it going to?" He had questioned, searchingly, prizing some emotion out of me that I was unable to give. I didn't have any answers, I was numb and even more so now that I was pregnant and unable to tell him we were going to have another baby, out of fear that he wouldn't be able to cope. I felt responsible and yet there wasn't a single part of me that felt it was wrong. Even if Mike and I didn't make it together, I knew I would strive with every part of my being to give my children the best that life had to offer. Even if that didn't involve material comforts, they would never lack in spiritual teachings and love. I surveyed my body in the full length mirror before pulling the bath robe around myself. Already I had gained a little weight, but I'd estimated I was about two months pregnant and I calculated in my mind the date of our baby's birth.

A sound from outside the doorway startled me. I wondered if Mike had forgotten something and come back. It was as if someone had walked across the landing and gone in to Annelleise's bedroom. I quickly pushed open the door to her room, feeling my heart beating fast. I stopped just inside the doorway, I could see her tucked in her bed, her mane of golden curls draped on to her pillow. Nothing was out of place. The softly ticking of her cuckoo clock was comforting in the stillness. I noticed her curtains were pulled only half way across. I smiled sensing Mike's presence in her room, how he and Annelleise loved to play together there.

I acknowledged the feeling of emptiness now he had gone but I pushed the apprehension deep down. The same beautiful, calm and living energy gathered, it was as if it was draping a shawl of warmth around my shoulders and I felt my breath heighten. I felt impressed to go in to our bedroom and collect my journal from beneath our bed, even though it had been several months since I had written in it. I left Annelleise's room, knowing she was protected and alright.

I noticed Mike's watch on his bedside table. I picked it up, feeling his warmth. His side was so neat and orderly, he hated that mine was always stacked with books and things which spoiled the overall appearance. I smiled feeling the ease and comfort of both our energies in our bed room and surveyed the journal in my hands. I didn't particularly feel like writing. If anything I was too tired. I opened the page of the last entry and saw that I'd written it after I'd last visited my parent's house some months earlier. Somehow since then, life had been too busy, too encroaching upon me to give me the space to let my thoughts have freedom from the demands of everyday life. Again, I thought of Mam and a feeling of deep sadness, registered in me, remembering my last heated conversation at their house about the dog, when my temper had boiled over and gotten the better of me and I'd screamed every four letter word under the sun at him and as I banged the door shut behind me, I vowed never to go back.

As I looked around and sensed the energies in the room, I felt somehow involved in some strange play of events, recombined in a perpetual sense of immanence of spiritual awakening. I wandered downstairs in to the living room and sat down on the sofa, opening my journal, as if in participatory expectation, of what, I wasn't sure. The clock's tick seemed louder, or was it just me, I wondered, as I registered at some interior level within, a heightening, which seemed to be felt inside my head, my whole body and everything around me. It was as though my hearing was amplified, at that moment it was as if everything, every tree and stone and hill, flower and river resonated with a sound, as if alive. I became aware of my breathing. It had become shallow and I had entered in to a meditative state of relaxation without even trying. This had happened so quickly, yet in the state of ordinary awareness, I think it was longer.

Almost at once, I became aware of someone sitting in the chair at the far side of the room, its presence was so purposeful, and I felt I was being observed by it and it unnerved me. Who was it? I listened to my inner voice ask. Part of me wanted to leave the room and hide, yet at the same time, I felt compelled to stay and relax. It felt as if there was energy moving between me and the Spirit, the distant sounds of the world, were no longer heard, there was just a silence and balance which was absorbed in the area around my heart. I felt unconditionally loved. I know that some will question these things, but I did. I was filled with joy and awareness, like so many times in my life before, when things had become too much, but this time, there was an inner certainty within me, that what I was experiencing was multidimensional and was of the Holy Spirit.

I closed my eyes, seeing only the faint lamp light behind my eye lids. At once, I became aware of a man in my mind's eye. I acknowledged it was the Spirit of the man who had been observing me. I trusted the energy immediately, as the bright magenta light flooded in to my third eye, as it had done my entire life, in moments like these. This time, however, it poured in to my head almost filling it up with a pulsating, moving energy. Each time it pulsated, more particles appeared to attach themselves to the inner light at the center and slowly but gradually it took on form.

At first the image was blurred and mutable, appearing to flow and change shape as it settled upon the inner core of my mind and then slowly, what looked like a plume of chalky substance appeared to form in the air and wrap itself around me. Part of me felt uneasy, I admit, as my mind raced to attempt to figure out what was happening to me. I attempted to move but felt rigid and steadfast in the chair, but my breathing was still very relaxed and my heart rate was steady. I certainly didn't feel afraid.

The time it took was probably no longer than thirty seconds in total, I can't be sure, when all at once, emerging from out of the plume of white chalky cloud, appeared a man of North American Indian origin, looking solid and real, with a single white feather visible from out of his thick black hair. With a rugged complexion and an offset nose, he attempted to smile at me through the plume of chalky vapor which seemed to now wrap itself around us both. I felt as if my heart ripped wide open at that moment with energy and love which poured forth from every part of my being and I felt such deep emotion for the man that tears flowed instantly. It was his eyes, deep set and alive with compassion and understanding that I recognized him, as he looked steadily at me. The recognition was so powerful, I knew him, but I didn't know how or where from.

All at once, I felt my body become weighty from my feet upwards and my limbs felt like they didn't belong to me, as a strange tingle of electricity coursed through my veins and my heart began to beat quickly. My hand gripped the pen and it took on a life of its own and I wrote speedily for a long time. It was as though I was aware of what I was writing and yet my mind was blank. I couldn't think of what I was trying to say and yet my hand continued to write the words. How long I was in that deep meditative state, I have no idea, for it was hours later that I awoke feeling cold with my journal beside me and the hands of the clock registered two am. I looked at the book I had written in, strewn with what looked like illegible writing, slanting across pages and pages. It didn't remotely resemble my own hand writing and I was certain it would be nothing more than jumbled words and letters.

How wrong I was. I began to read it, with some difficulty, at first, because the words appeared to have been written shakily and there was no punctuation so it wasn't easy to see where the sentence stopped and another started. It soon became apparent upon reading that it wasn't written in the first person, in other words, I hadn't written it, at least not in the sense of my usual journal style. A part of me felt a little afraid, remembering how I had felt myself becoming weighted down and my hand had held the pen and had written as if without my intention. Yet evidently it was benign, loving and supportive. Greeting me as if being reunited again, after years of long absence and urging me with such devoted compassion to explore the nature of the things which were written and test the theories given, but at a pace that was embracing of my own needs in life. It spoke so factually about the difficulties in my relationships and how I would benefit from learning how to meditate properly to restore vital energies. Perhaps even more compelling was the way in which it talked about Mike and me, as though it knew of the struggles we were encountering on a daily basis and appreciated how hard life had become for us both, but more dismayingly, about the struggles that lay ahead, that no matter how difficult they'd be, we would have to face.

I cried, feeling as if I'd been comforted by a loving parent. I couldn't know then as I sat that morning in the early twilight, how that writing was just the start, only the beginning of a journey I'd take with Spirit, my Guide and Inspirers, as an instrument for them, transcribing their teachings about life and love and the continuance and existence of the soul upon death of the physical body. That I would be taken to realms where I'd meet loved ones again and encounter the spirit of friends that I would eventually meet on Earth. 'White Feather', I believe, chose that moment in my life, to awaken me fully to the reality of his presence and to the Spirit World, to aid me at a time which was so critical and important in the shaping and development of the future for Mike, me and our children. To help us to make positive choices that would lead to a happier and more fulfilling life, and also for me to learn how to utilize the energies within me to help others through Complementary Holistic Medicine and healing.

In the years that followed, the sittings with White Feather were to become a life line in times of intense and critical loneliness, offering love, guidance and support. For in their spiritual higher wisdom and omnipotent understanding, they knew of the difficulties that lay ahead and the devastating losses that were to come, that no amount of love in the world would be enough to hold Mike and me together. A bridge would form between us, one that Mike would choose to cross, where contact between us would cease as he walked away from the past and his children. For well over a decade, their attempts to contact him would be rebuffed. It was a period in time of catastrophic sadness, as together we endured the sorrows from that loss. However, the blossoming and growing through such experiences, would also prove to be the strengthening and molding of our characters and as the years unfolded the only path to follow, was the path of love.

*'Human beings are at times like eternal children in awe and wonder in the candy store of their world. Whatever looks colourful must be delicious and therefor greatly desired.*

*Whatever ingenuity projected forth in technology, must indeed be their greatest prize, to own, display and base their whole lives upon. They seldom realize what it is that they base their rationalities upon, for if they did, realism of such would quicken them in to self-realization and ultimate change.*

*This is a certainty transcending all, an unparalleled truth which releases humans from the bondage of the material world. But what if change is prevented by the refusal to accept that notion?*

*What if human beings continue to grasp on to the rope they have known to be their security, until the rope grows thin, as each concept of that security reduces it to a single thread and it snaps right at the center of a life crisis?*

*The rope, of course is merely symbolic of the deeper roots to which he/she has attached themselves.*

*Just as surely as they believe that their only worthwhile pursuit is physical in orientation, they have already reduced their sense of security and why? Because that security is created out of the faith in the rope and the rope is not physical at all.*

*So what perpetuates or initiates change? For most, it is the inability to withstand any further difficulty, likened to a draining in the sense of the body's defenses to cope with any further onslaught of trauma; a yielding as it were, to remove oneself from the deep seated pain.*

*But often even at these times, human beings still reckon on the physical pleasures as a way to temporarily numb their pain or at best, escape from it.*

*And so they reach out in to the world, for yet more pleasurable ways in which to uplift the mind and body. On and on it goes, endlessly in the course of the life, never questioning to find out why the problem keeps arising or why the conditions remain the same.*

*Human beings are only in a state of perpetual imprisonment as long as they themselves believe this to be so. It is conscious thought. They have forgotten that their creative powers are genius and for many, this concept was never a part of their early teaching. The creativity of a human being is un-likened to all else, save the creative process of life itself, but even then, human beings are a part of that whole process.*

*And so it is with 'Love' which is the cause of great strife for many in the physical world. There is little understanding of the true meaning. In the span of life, souls strive for the perfect love and thus experience the greatest of pain.*

*Human beings seek to know it, in terms of words and symbol, ever finding expression for the written word. Love is empty of words, for it is the emotional counterpart of the creative element of grace. It is the opening of the 'Soul' in connection with the 'Divine'.*

*'Divine Grace' bestows upon all of life, the generative spark that which we call 'Love', for in reality it is 'Universal-Love', and part of which human beings are and always have been, and though they think in terms of limits and bounds, there are no such limits and bounds in reality.*

*'Devotion' and a gentle appeal to care and a desire to create 'Peace' is all that is necessary and is thus on every level pertaining to 'Love'.*

*You are loved unconditionally, now and forever".*

(White Feather)